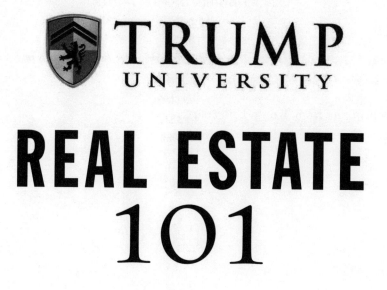

REAL ESTATE
101

OTHER BOOKS IN THE TRUMP
UNIVERSITY SERIES

Trump University Marketing 101: How to Use the Most Powerful Ideas in Marketing to Get More Customers

Forthcoming from Trump University
Trump University Entrepreneurship 101

TRUMP
UNIVERSITY

REAL ESTATE
101

Building Wealth with
Real Estate Investments

GARY W. ELDRED, PhD
FOREWORD BY DONALD TRUMP

WILEY

JOHN WILEY & SONS, INC.

For general information on our other products and services or for technical support, please contact our Customer Care Department within the United States at (800) 762–2974, outside the United States at (317) 572–3993 or fax (317) 572–4002.

Wiley also publishes its books in a variety of electronic formats. Some content that appears in print may not be available in electronic books. For more information about Wiley products, visit our web site at www.wiley.com.

ISBN 13: 978–0–471–91727–4
ISBN 10: 0–471–91727–3

Printed in the United States of America.

10 9 8 7 6 5 4

CONTENTS

CONTENTS

ACKNOWLEDGMENTS

I WISH TO thank Donald Trump and Michael Sexton, CEO, Trump University, for inviting me to become the content expert for their real estate mastery program. Mr. Trump has said on many occasions, "I only hire the best." That's certainly true for the team at Trump University, and I am honored by their request to join them.

Specifically, in working on this book, I want to thank my colleague in the UAE, Zouheir Jarkas, whose work and assistance has proved invaluable. I would also like to recognize my assistant, Omer Shabbir Ahmed, who not only went beyond the call of duty to help me meet deadlines but also produced work of the highest quality. Mohsen Mofid has also helped, and I thank him for his continued efforts.

Foreword to the Trump University 101 Series

by Donald J. Trump

People often ask me the secret to my success, and the answer is simple: focus, hard work, and tenacity. I've had some lucky breaks, but luck will only get you so far. You also need business savvy—not necessarily a degree from Wharton, but you do need the desire and discipline to educate yourself. I created Trump University to give motivated business people the skills required to achieve lasting success.

The Trump University 101 Series explains the most powerful and important ideas in business—the same concepts taught in the most respected MBA curriculums and used by the most successful companies in the world, including The Trump Organization. Each book is written by a top professor, author, or entrepreneur whose goal is to help you put these ideas to use in your business right away. If you're not satisfied with the status quo in your career, read this book, pick one key idea, and implement it. I guarantee it will make you money.

Donald Trump congratulates Gary Eldred for his oustanding work on Trump University's mastery program in real estate. (Photo by Karen Slavick, Trump University)

1

Entrepreneuring in Real Estate with
Donald Trump

IN THIS BOOK, you will discover the principles of entrepreneuring in real estate as lived and practiced by the ultimate entrepreneur, Mr. Donald Trump. Mr. Trump's entry into the field of entrepreneurial education stands as a welcome and needed change.

Now, more than ever, Mr. Trump's wisdom is needed. Because as many property markets throughout the United States and around the world begin to simmer rather than boil, we are returning to an arena where winning in the game of property will require much more than luck and fortuitous timing. We are once again moving into a market where investors must create value, not just reap windfall gains.

As Mr. Trump told me when we were planning this book, "For all too long, the infomercial guys of late night television who promote 'nothing down,' 'pennies on the dollar foreclosures,' 'quick flipping,' and other supposed techniques to 'get rich quick' have dominated the field of real estate books and tapes." Then he added, "Life rarely works out that way. If you go for get rich quick, you are really going for broke."

We don't want you to go broke—or go for broke. We aren't going to promise you that following the entrepreneurial principles of Donald Trump and Gary Eldred will turn you into an overnight millionaire.

We do, however, promise that our principles will help you build wealth, achieve your personal potential, and create value for your customers. Even better, like us, you just might have a lot of fun along the way.

Indeed, our philosophy of entrepreneuring in real estate doesn't just apply to property or building wealth. You can apply it to live a richer, fuller life in every respect. "Think big, live large." With that now famous motto, Mr. Trump encourages you to "see each day as an important day for your future and a special day just because you have it. You will energize your existence. 'What a great day!' Say it right now and feel the positive thinking it generates. Give yourself a chance to do your best, and everyone will benefit. Know that you can fill today with possibilities and opportunities."

In sum, here is the basic mindfulness that powers Mr. Trump's philosophy and, accordingly, his life. In later chapters, we will show you in detail how this philosophy can lead you to the life you want.

OPEN YOUR MIND TO POSSIBILITIES

To achieve your potential, educate yourself to think and expand your possibilities. It turns out that both Mr. Trump and I began reading books on real estate while we were undergraduates in college. Both of us began investing in property when nearly all of our fellow students were more interested in buying a sharp car and finding a cool apartment to rent.

Why did we act differently? Why did we begin to build wealth at an age when most people come up with multiple excuses? Because we refused to accept the conventional wisdom that we were too young, too inexperienced, or too anything else.

Yes, Mr. Trump came from a relatively well-off family (as I did not). But that wasn't the difference. Most students at Penn came from well-off families. A big difference then and today is that both of us achieve more than our peers because we continuously open our minds to new ideas. Nay, we continuously search out new ideas and information. Both of us are big readers—to learn about the world at large and about real estate—and we are big readers in the field (for the lack of a better term) of self-help psychology.

In this book, we hope that by reminding and encouraging you to think positively, create possibilities, and open your horizons, you too will become more of what you would like to become.

KNOW THE DETAILS

Opening your mind to possibilities opens your mind to profits. But positive (I like to say exploratory) thinking won't count for much if you don't prime yourself with an ever-growing flow of knowledge. As Mr. Trump likes to say, "I'm not young enough to know everything."

Indeed, he keeps Kipling's six honest men ever present to build his knowledge. Their names are What, Why, When, How, Where, and Who.

"To get a building built in New York City," says Mr. Trump, "requires knowledge of zoning, contractors, architects, air rights, tax laws, unions, and a thousand other things—not least of which are the intended customers. When I started, I had to learn a lot. No one else could learn it for me. But every day, I would learn something, apply it, and make progress. Believe me, becoming a developer didn't happen overnight.

"If I had started in business thinking I knew everything, I'd been finished before I got started. Avoid that mistake. Real estate includes many hidden details.

"I always warn people not to jump into anything unprepared. It's that old fine line between bravery and stupidity. Know the tides before you dive in. There's always a certain amount of danger, danger meaning the unknown, even in shallow waters. Riptides and sharks live there. Sometimes you don't see them until it's too late. Keep that in mind no matter how sensational or foolproof you think your idea might be.

"In those early years, I spent a great deal of time researching every detail that might be pertinent to the deal I was interested in making. I still do the same today. People often comment on how quickly I operate, but the reason I can move quickly is that I've done the background work first, which no one usually sees. I prepare myself thoroughly. Then, when it is time to move ahead, I am ready to sprint."

THINK FOR YOURSELF—ACCEPT RESPONSIBILITY

You will need to incorporate the facts and opinions of others into your investment decisions but never abdicate your decisions to your advisers.

"This issue is serious for worldly as well as personal reasons," says Mr. Trump. "The worst things in history have happened when people stop thinking for themselves, especially when they allow themselves to be influenced by negative people. That's what gives rise to dictators. Avoid that error at all costs. Stop it first on a personal level, and you will have contributed to world sanity as well as your own.

"You need a mind-set of personal responsibility. When I say to have the right mind-set, I am thinking about responsibility. People who take responsibility have no need to blame others or to be continually finding fault. The naysayers never manage to contribute much and never amount to much either. Don't join their club. They're the lowest common denominator.

"I knew a guy that I used to call up just to see who and what he would be *blaming* that day. I don't think that guy ever thought he had personally made a single mistake in his entire life. From day one, nothing was ever his fault. His biggest blind spot was himself, and, sad to say, he eventually became a total loser because he never thought of the remedy for his biggest failure: himself. Look at yourself first when things go wrong.

"I've been in business long enough now and have had ups and downs, so I can go from seeing the problem to seeing the solution rather quickly. Don't emphasize the problem so much—emphasize the solution. It's a mind-set that works: Accentuate the positive without being blind to the negative. It's your responsibility!"

GOALS AND HABITS

"Give your goals substance," advises Mr. Trump. "Imbue them with a value that exceeds the monetary. Make them count on as many levels as you can. Give them a subtext that will provide them with a dimension that will benefit not only you but other people as well. That's an important aspect of thinking big—and a big step toward greater success.

After a while, people will know you by your habits and your habitual behavior. These habits can be qualities, as Aristotle points out. If your behavior is consistently of a high standard, your particular quality may be integrity. So review your habits and make sure they are leading you in the right direction. Make sure you are working toward the result you want to see and know that your way of achieving them will be distinctly your way. Define your own boundaries, your own goals, without being influenced negatively by anyone else."

The Art of the Deal

You must put yourself into your deals. You must commit. Mr. Trump likes to quote Thoreau's passage: "I know of no more encouraging fact than the unquestioned ability of a man to elevate his life by conscious desire." That is not only an encouraging statement but also an empowering one. It means that you can accomplish a lot by applying your brainpower and then moving forward with it. Thought without action won't amount to much in the long run. Those great ideas you have will remain stillborn unless you actively do something with them.

So let's get started. We're going to give you some empowering knowledge. Put that knowledge into action. Become your best.

2

You Can Still Achieve Wealth in Real Estate

> **I love Rudyard Kipling's "Six honest men." Their names are "What and Why and When—and How, Where, and Who." Ask questions.**

I LOVE REAL ESTATE. And I hope that by the time you complete this book, you will too.

Real estate offers more people more opportunities than any other type of investment. Great economy, poor economy, high interest rates, low interest rates, boom market, bust market—it makes no difference. I have made money through all types of markets and economic conditions. And so will you—if you learn to think and act as a real estate entrepreneur. Achieving wealth, personal independence, and financial freedom requires only two basic conditions:

1. Guide your daily life with an entrepreneurial mind-set, character, and action plan.
2. Apply a systematic possibility-driven method to discover, create, and harvest real estate value.

THINK AND ACT AS AN ENTREPRENEUR

Popular culture frequently mischaracterizes the entrepreneur. For many people, the entrepreneur represents the brash, bold risk taker who charges ahead come hell or high water. He's often pictured as a promoter who slick-sells hype over substance. In this warped scene, greed motivates base behavior. This "entrepreneur" will do or say almost anything to make a quick buck.

Undoubtedly, the real estate business attracts more than its share of practitioners and gurus who more or less reinforce this dark perception. In stark contrast, at Trump University, our view of entrepreneurs aligns with a passage from a speech that the late President Ronald Reagan delivered in 1985 at St. John's University.

"We have lived through the age of big industry and the age of the giant corporation," Mr. Reagan said, "but I believe this is the age of the entrepreneur. . . . That's where American prosperity is coming from now, and that's where it's going to come from in the future."

The ultimate resource—as economics Professor Julian Simon emphasizes in his book by the same title—is people. Professor Simon proves that we need not worry about running out of oil, coal, or, for that matter, land. As long as there are people who demonstrate the "can do" spirit and as long as people grow their creative abilities to solve problems, we can look to a bright future. "The main fuel to speed our progress," Professor Simon concludes, "is our stock of knowledge, and the brake is our lack of imagination. The ultimate resource is people—skilled, spirited, and hopeful people who will exert their wills and imagination for their own benefits, and for the benefit of us all."

Don't lose focus of the big picture. Entrepreneurs need a clear-cut purpose to achieve success.

So here's our Trump University pledge: If you choose to go into real estate, if you choose to motivate your life with an entrepreneurial spirit, you will enjoy unlimited opportunity to work for your own benefit, for the benefit of those you serve, and, through responsible, ethical behavior, for the benefit of us all. By combining knowledge, effort, and imagination, you will create real estate value.

Know that life is like an act; perform to the best of your ability to successfully captivate your audience.

Entrepreneurial Thinking vs. Motivated Sellers

Entrepreneurial thinking differs from most widely touted real estate advice. Most "get rich in real estate" books preach the gospel of motivated sellers. They tell you that to seek your fortune in property, find motivated sellers—those desperate souls plagued by divorce, layoffs, credit card debt, medical bills, foreclosure, and bankruptcy.

According to the gurus who tout this approach to profit, such troubled folks will gladly sell you their property for 20, 30, maybe 40 percent below its market value. You enjoy instant equity.

Does this technique work? Yes, on occasion. But without a doubt, the gurus overstate its promise and understate its shortcomings in three ways: through violations of ethics and law, practical difficulties, and stunted entrepreneurial vision.

Violations of Ethics and Law

When many investors negotiate with troubled sellers, they overstep ethical and moral boundaries. They pressure, deceive, and make promises that they do not intend to keep. In fact, to combat such unethical practices, many states have now enacted laws that specifically regulate sales by motivated sellers in foreclosure. Although entrepreneurs do sometimes negotiate with troubled, motivated sellers, when doing so, they tread lightly with full, honest disclosure.

Practical Difficulties

The motivated seller approach adds practical difficulty to the issue of ethics. You cannot easily find motivated sellers with substantial amounts of equity who will sell to you at a price substantially below market value. It happens. But it takes work. My Trump University audio-workbook, *The Real Estate Goldmine*, captures my view of this approach to real estate profits. As with a gold mine, you find your nuggets of gold only through persistent and tough digging.

Stunted Entrepreneurial Vision

Clearly, ethical, legal, and practical difficulties make motivated sellers a tough row to hoe. But more to my point, the focus on motivated sellers has stunted the entrepreneurial vision of two generations of investors. I have heard or read this advice hundreds of times: "Never buy any property unless you can get it for at least 20 percent under market." Balderdash. To make a sound decision, you need to figure out the *total* profit potential of a property.

Yes, by all means, when it makes ethical and economic sense, search for and negotiate a bargain price. Ferret out those motivated sellers whom you can help resolve their most pressing concerns. But do not let this one technique blur your creative vision. Always add in potential profits from cash flow, appreciation potential, terms and costs of financing, mortgage payoff, and, most significantly, opportunities for adding value to the property.

As an entrepreneur, you will find profits lurking in dozens of hiding places when you sharpen your vision to see them.

Don't let anyone tell you that you can't price yourself higher than the competition. We break the comps on all of our projects.

Entrepreneurial Thinking vs. Property Appreciation

Whereas many property gurus wrongly claim that motivated sellers offer you the best chance to achieve wealth through real estate, the financial press seems obsessed with property appreciation. According to hundreds of articles that have appeared of late, real estate has appreciated too fast, for too long. Thus, investors should look for other ways to make money. Not only does the future look bleak for price increases, but, more dangerously, they say, when the property bubble bursts, investors and home owners will lose their shirts. "Sell now!" chant many so-called economic experts.

So let's address these two issues:

1. Do you need market appreciation to build wealth in real estate?
2. Should you fear a property bubble?

As you will see, entrepreneurs answer each of these questions with a resounding No!

Do You Need Market Appreciation?

In the fast-moving property markets of the early 2000s, investors, home owners, and speculators made bundles of money from property appreciation. That's great. But this experience has generated a logical fallacy; that is, that without appreciation, profits languish. You might as well put your money into a savings account: less risk, greater expected return.

Fortunately, this bleak assessment ignores three other major sources of real estate profit: cash flow, amortization (mortgage payoff), and value creation. For now, let's focus on cash flow and mortgage payoff. We will discuss value creation later.

I began my investing in a no-growth town in Indiana. One of my first properties cost $100,000. I paid $10,000 down, and the seller financed the balance over 10 years. This older (I should say aged) apartment building did not appreciate. After 12 years, I sold it for $100,000, the same price I had paid.[1]

To the appreciation addict, it may seem that my apartment building proved to be a lousy investment. A closer look at the numbers reveals a bonanza.

After operating expenses and debt service, that property netted $2,500 a year in after-tax cash flow. Just in terms of cash flow, I earned an annual return on my $10,000 cash invested of 25 percent. In addition, that $10,000 down payment grew to a total equity of $100,000 (recall, I paid the note off at year 10).

Without appreciation, without value-creating improvements, I earned a total annual rate of return in excess of 30 percent. Can you still buy such properties? Yes, even today you can find similarly attractive deals in some parts of the South and Midwest.

Never singularly focus only on appreciation. Just as the "dogs of the Dow" sometimes outperform the Microsofts and Amazons, so too can out-of-favor, no- or slow-growth property markets offer highly attractive yields. The entrepreneur knows that he or she

---

[1] For ease of illustration, this example uses rounded numbers.

can achieve strong returns even in those times or areas where price increases take a long vacation.

Should You Fear a Property Bubble?

In another note to discourage, the press repeatedly hypes the so-called property bubble. But, before you imbibe this babble about a property bubble, before you fall into a paralyzing funk of negativity, place today's bleak forecasts within a historical context. For the past 60 years, economists, Wall Street analysts, and other supposed financial experts have wrongly predicted the end of real estate. Take a quick trip through their far-off-the-mark forecasts from years gone by:

- "The prices of houses seem to have reached a plateau, and there is reasonable expectancy that prices will decline." (*Time*, December 1, 1947)
- "Houses cost too much for the mass market. Today's average price is around $8,000—out of reach for two-thirds of all buyers." (*Science Digest*, April 1948)
- "If you have bought your house since the War. . . . you have made your deal at the top of the market. . . . The days when you couldn't lose on a house purchase are no longer with us." (*House Beautiful*, November 1948)
- "The goal of owning a home seems to be getting beyond the reach of more and more Americans. The typical new house today costs $28,000." (*Business Week*, September 4, 1969)
- "Be suspicious of the 'common wisdom' that tells you to 'Buy now. . . . because continuing inflation will force home prices and rents higher and higher.'" (*NEA Journal*, December 1970)
- "In California. . . . for example, it is not unusual to find families of average means buying $100,000 houses. . . . I'm confident prices have passed their peak." (John Wesley English and Gray Emerson Cardiff, *The Coming Real Estate Crash*, 1980)
- "The era of easy profits in real estate may be drawing to a close." (*Money*, January 1981)

- "The golden-age of risk-free run-ups in home prices is gone." (*Money*, March 1985)
- "If you're looking to buy, be careful. Rising home values are not a sure thing anymore." (*Miami Herald*, October 25, 1985)
- "Most economists agree. . . . [a home] will become little more than a roof and a tax deduction, certainly not the lucrative investment it was through much of the 1980s." (*Money*, April 1986)
- "The baby boomers are all housed now. They are being followed by the baby bust. By 2005, real housing prices will sit 40 percent below where they are today." (Harvard economist Gregory Mankiw, "The Baby Boom, the Baby Bust, and the Coming Collapse of Housing Prices," *Journal of Regional Economics*, Fall 1989)
- "We're starting to go back to the time when you bought a home not for its potential money-making abilities, but rather as a nesting spot." (*Los Angeles Times*, January 31, 1993)
- "Financial planners agree that houses will continue to be a poor investment." (*Kiplinger's Personal Financial Magazine*, November 1993)
- "A home is where the bad investment is." (*San Francisco Examiner*, November 17, 1996)
- "Your house is a roof over your head. It is not an investment." (*Everything You Know about Money Is Wrong*, 2000)
- "But the real question is, how will [housing prices] look longer term? As I've said in the past, I do not think that housing values will be higher five to ten years from now." (Yale economist Robert Shiller, quoted in *Newsweek*, January 27, 2005)

Now think ahead. Who enjoys the highest net worth today? Those fear-induced folks who believed the press pundits and pontificators of yesteryear? Or those property entrepreneurs who ignored the know-nothing naysayers and proceeded to acquire properties through both up and down markets?

Most importantly, 10, 15, or 20 years from now, who will enjoy the highest net worths and greatest degree of financial freedom? Those who follow the Chicken Little articles and books babbling about the bubble? Or those who follow the entrepreneurial principles and philosophy of Donald Trump and Gary Eldred?

Caution: Our principles do not tell you to buy anything, at any price, at any time—although history even proves that that unthinking strategy would generally have yielded good returns. And yes, some (but certainly not most) property markets show wide cyclical ups and downs (with each new up surpassing former peaks). Yes, most often, great deals require work and creativity. Yes, sometimes you might get caught in an unexpected downdraft. But these facts miss the point.

All types of property markets, economic conditions, and even serious difficulties present entrepreneurial opportunities for profit. Donald Trump began his career in the dark years of the mid-1970s, when virtually no one wanted to buy or develop property in the near bankrupt New York City. Even more impressive, Mr. Trump sowed the seeds for his present prosperity during his loan workout days of the early 1990s—surely a strong example of turning lemons into lemonade.

So we invite you to choose: Will you accept fear-mongering forecasts—forecasts that have perpetually erred? Will you imbibe cliché and half-baked conventional wisdom? Or will you ignore the whirlwind of bubble babble to become a real estate entrepreneur? Will you look beyond the journalistic pundits and economic experts to trust the voice of reason, hope, and experience? In other words, will you let fear and a lack of knowledge keep you benched on the sidelines of prosperity? Or will you choose to control your own life and actively navigate toward the financial and personal destiny that you would like to achieve?

If you answer, "Yes! Sign me up. I'm coming on board," good for you. In the pages that follow, you will discover the road to wealth and financial freedom. Let us show you how to think and act as a real estate entrepreneur—someone who can see a seedy hotel located in a deteriorating neighborhood yet envision a Grand Hyatt Hotel surrounded by upscale shops, restaurants, and cafés, someone who can see site zoning rules that restrict a building to a height of 40 stories yet obtain legal approval to build New York City's tallest mixed-use structure of luxury condominiums of 80 stories (twice the height seemingly written into law).

As a knowledgeable, motivated entrepreneur, you will put together like-kind deals. They may not rival these Trump deals in size or amount. But all the same, they will engage your power to imagine, create, and build a better life for others—and yourself.

3

How to Become a Real Estate Entrepreneur

When I began working with Donald Trump, I was pleased to learn that he shares my passion for reading. But even more surprising (although upon reflection, it shouldn't have been), Mr. Trump shares my belief in the value of psychology, and, for lack of a better term, self-help books.

One of Mr. Trumps favorite sayings is "your attitude determines your altitude." Unfortunately, most so-called experts in the field of academic finance and investments dismiss such advice as mere "pop psychology." To the professors, successful investing only requires skill with numbers and quantitative methods. In fact, until recently, university business schools did not teach even one course in behavioral finance—a field that has captured a Nobel prize.

As Mr. Trump has said, "In business school, I would not have believed psychology could contribute to financial success." In fact, success begins not with knowledge per se, but with the "castles your mind builds." Without the right habits of mind and corresponding habits of action, no would-be entrepreneur is likely to accomplish much. To Mr. Trump, the characteristics that lead to success include the following:

1. *Think positively:* It's your choice. You can find excuses or you can accept responsibility. You can find those who will complain with you. Or you can surround yourself with people who believe in what you (and they) can do, not what you can't do. Your attitude gives wings to your wants and goals.

2. *Don't do it (just for) the money:* "Choose your goals so that you can pursue them with passion and enthusiasm," says Mr. Trump. "You will hit tough times. Your passion and enthusiasm will keep your momentum. Your passion and enthusiasm, your sense of accomplishment will get you over, around, under, or through those brick walls that will undoubtedly stand in your way. With enthusiasm, problems provide you a challenge, not a reason to quit."

3. *Set the standard:* "Ask yourself," says Mr. Trump. "What standards would you like to be known for? What standards will exceed what

your customers want? My father set great standards for his bread and butter houses and apartments. When I built Trump Tower, it opened to wonderful reviews, and established itself as a landmark building. Like my father, I set and then surpassed my standards, and in a big way."

Today, Mr. Trump continues to set new, high standards, not just with luxury buildings, but also with his golf courses. One leading golfing magazine has written that Mr. Trump "settles for nothing less than the best. If he puts his name on it, it's got to be great. Trump's first two golf course 'masterpieces'—Trump International at Mar-a-Lago in South Florida and Trump National in Westchester County, N.Y.—are undeniably great. They've won the awards and converted the naysayers. And he's already gone on record with hopes of someday bringing the U.S. Open to his new course in Bedminster, N.J., which is built on the former estate of auto magnate John DeLorean."

Simply stated, these three Trump principles will guide your entrepreneurial success: (1) develop and nurture positive habits of mind, (2) enjoy the money, but motivate yourself with passion and enthusiasm, and (3) set the standard that pleases yourself, your customers, and forces others to follow.

I'm not young enough to know everything. I'm always asking questions.

HISTORY PROVES THAT even average mom-and-pop property investors have achieved returns that would make the manager of a superstar mutual fund drool with envy. The more than 30 percent return that I earned on my first apartment building did not represent anything out of the ordinary. As you recall, my gain with that property occurred without price appreciation or value creation. In fact, during my early years as an investor, I mostly milked my properties for cash flow to support myself during college and graduate school.

My Entrepreneurial Awakening

Luckily, after completing my Ph.D., my entrepreneurial vision broadened. Through a referral from the dean of the business school where I was teaching finance and real estate, I got involved in property development. In addition, I landed a plum consulting assignment on a property deal for Roger Miliken (a Forbes 400 billionaire).

These experiences opened my eyes. Although my property investments paid off nicely, I soon recognized that an entrepreneurial approach to real estate can pay much larger dividends than anything I had previously imagined.

As Charlie Frazier (the original developer of Sea Pines Plantation on Hilton Head) once told me, "You can make money with real estate, but you can make far more with your ideas. My balance sheet shows property is my largest asset. But that's wrong for me and it's wrong for you. Your mind holds far more promise and potential than this entire island [Hilton Head] we're standing on."

Since those days in South Carolina, I've met and become friends with many more top-level entrepreneurs—some you've probably heard of, such as Mary Kay Ash, Ebby Halliday, Mark Victor Hansen, Frank McKinney, Trammel Crow, and, of course, Donald Trump. Others lead less visible lives, much like those profiled in *The Millionaire Next Door* (by Thomas Stanley).

Mind over Matter

Although each of these entrepreneurs differs in style and personality, every single one has emphasized to me the critical importance of mind over matter.

Cosmetics did not make Mary Kay Ash wealthy. Mary Kay happened to earn her wealth through cosmetics (actually by creating a world-class sales organization). Textiles did not make Roger Miliken wealthy. Roger Miliken happened to build his wealth through textiles. Property did not make Donald Trump wealthy. Donald Trump happened to build his wealth through property. Do you see what I'm saying? Entrepreneurs succeed because of the principles and philosophy they rely on to guide their lives—not the particular product or industry per se.

> **Compete with yourself to be the best you can.**
> **Entrepreneurs know that competing with others**
> **lowers their standards.**

Donald Trump and I do favor property. But we do not want you to believe that property can make you wealthy (although it might). We urge you to think, "I can create wealth through property." Entrepreneurs stress active personal control and responsibility.

Magnify Your Favorable Odds

Does an entrepreneurial approach guarantee success in every endeavor? Of course not. That's precisely why entrepreneurs differ from the majority. Few of us get through life without hard knocks. But the entrepreneurial approach offers the principles and philosophy necessary to bounce back.

> **Encountering an obstacle doesn't necessarily mean**
> **going through it; you can try going around, under,**
> **or over it. I never give up until I've exhausted all of**
> **my possibilities.**

Even though an entrepreneurial outlook does not guarantee universal success, it sure magnifies the odds in your favor.

With 25 years of experience in real estate and other ventures, I can look back for a postmortem diagnosis of my own screw-ups. Each and every time I let "misfortune" get the better of me, I violated a key entrepreneurial principle. More distressing, I now see that within the center of such storms lies an eye of opportunity that I missed because of "woe is me" confusion. This malady in turn blocked my ability to imagine and execute multiple optimistic outcomes.

Guide Your Life with Entrepreneurial Principles

Lest I sound maudlin, I am pleased to report that, like Donald Trump, overall my life has been blessed with good fortune. Both of us have experienced far more successes than setbacks. And we are convinced that if you adopt our entrepreneurial principles and philosophy as your own, you too can take your personal and financial life to a much higher level of satisfaction and wealth (while avoiding some of the mistakes that each of us has made.)

So here's our thoughts on how you can become a top-gun real estate entrepreneur:

1. Elevate your attitudes.
2. Program your positive self-talk.
3. Dig your well before you're thirsty.
4. Curtail your destructive spending and borrowing.
5. Plan your time, shape your life.
6. Honor your appointments, promises, and agreements.
7. Learn continuously, improve continuously.
8. Make great decisions.

Want proof that these principles work? Just look around you. Who are the people who live the most emotionally satisfying, prosperous, and financially independent lives? I will wager that they are the people who find ways to move forward rather mire themselves in complaint. They are the people who do what they plan and plan what they do. They see possibilities when others see obstacles. These skills begin with attitude.

Elevate Your Attitudes

"Your attitude determines your altitude." To achieve large goals, think positive, think big. It's the mind-set that speakers such as Donald Trump, Zig Ziglar, Tony Robbins, and Les Brown prescribe for their audiences. Do not dismiss the power of positive attitude as mere pop psychology. Today, no one can seriously question the power of positive attitude to bring welcome and lasting change to your life.

> **There have been so many books and examples about the power of positive thinking that it seems unnecessary to even mention it. Yet, I still see examples every single day of the power that negative thinking has over people. So, either people haven't gotten the message or they're just plain not paying attention. I hope that doesn't include any of you, because I don't have much tolerance for that kind of attitude.**

In the field of medicine, for example, Dr. David Burns has scientifically pioneered the practice of cognitive therapy to help patients develop positive attitudes and beliefs that help them conquer debilitating depression. (See his best-selling book, *Feeling Good*.) "As a man thinketh, so shall he live" even formed the theme of self-help books published in the 1800s. Both science and the test of time prove that positive attitudes improve performance. We live as creatures of habit, but we form habits through our prevalent and persistent attitudes and beliefs.

You've heard people say, "I'll believe it when I see it." Psychologist Dr. Wayne Dyer turns that phrase around to say, "You'll see it when you believe it." In fact, as Dr. Dyer points out, believing that you can achieve the goals you want spurs you to find ways to realize them. It stands to reason that if you fail to believe that you can realize your chosen goals, you'll never try.

During the mid-1990s, I conducted a national seminar program called Stop Renting Now! In personal conversation with seminar attendees, I learned that negative attitudes and beliefs had vanquished their dreams of home ownership far more than the lack of credit, income, or cash. Most people could have owned years before I met them. (Surprisingly, these folks were not in their 20s, as I expected they would be. Rather, most were over age 35.) Because they falsely believed that they could not own, they never searched out the knowledge that would have opened their eyes. Blinded by distorted beliefs, they could not see their actual possibilities. To counter this disabling affliction, I titled the first chapter of my book "Yes! You Can Own the Home You Want, 'Attitude + Education = Homeowner.'"

Your attitudes and beliefs do determine your altitude. Drs. David Burns and Wayne Dyer are right. You will see it when you believe it. Set your goals high. Then, through knowledge and education, figure out a way to conquer your obstacles and challenges. Entrepreneurs think positive and big. What do you want?

Program Your Positive Self-Talk

What do you say when you talk to yourself? Do you frequently chastise yourself yet at the same time relinquish responsibility for your own behavior? Do you find yourself saying anything similar to the following?

- I can't remember names.
- It's going to be another one of those days!
- It's just no use!
- I just know it won't work!
- That's just my luck.
- I don't have the talent.
- I'm just not creative.
- I can't seem to get organized.
- Today just isn't my day!
- I can never afford the things I want.
- No matter what I do, I can't seem to lose weight.
- I never have enough time.
- I just don't have the patience for that.
- I never know what to say.
- With my luck, I don't have a chance!
- I'd like to stop smoking, but I can't seem to quit.
- Things just aren't working out for me.
- I don't have the energy I used to.
- I'm really out of shape.
- I never have any money left over at the end of the month.
- Why should I try; it's not going to work anyway!
- I've never been any good at that.
- Nobody wants to pay me what I'm worth.
- I'm just no good at math.
- I lose weight, but then I gain it right back again.
- I just can't seem to get anything done!
- I'm just not a salesman.
- I always freeze up in front of a group.
- I get a cold this time every year.
- I'm just not cut out for that.
- I never seem to get anyplace on time.
- If only I had more time.
- If only I had more money.

If any of these (or similar) self-put-downs ring true, you're programming yourself to fail. In his excellent book *What to Say When You Talk to Yourself*, Dr. Shad Helmstetter writes,

> You will become what you think about most. Your success or failure in anything, large or small, will depend on your programming—what you accept from others and what you say when you talk to yourself. . . . The more you think about anything in a certain way, the more you will feel that belief accurately reflects reality.

Have you let the following (or similar) types of self-talk stifle your wealth-building possibility thinking?

- I should have invested earlier; interest rates are heading back up.
- I'll never be able to come up with the cash necessary to invest.
- There's no way we can cut our spending. We're going without now.
- Property is no longer a good investment.
- The world is full of haves and have-nots. I'm a have-not.
- At these prices, it's cheaper to rent than own.
- There's not anything out there I like that I can afford.
- My credit score is too low.
- My bills are too high.
- Our generation has it tougher than those who came before us.
- None of my friends has money to invest.
- It's too late. People who bought earlier were lucky.
- I hesitate to invest. I hardly know the first thing about it.
- I don't know any real estate agents, loan reps, or investors.
- Sure, I would like to buy property, but I don't have the money.
- Sure, I would like to invest *someday*.

This list could continue. You might add a few possibility stifling excuses of your own. It's all too easy to get caught in a self-defeating cycle. To a certain extent, negative reporting by much of the media programs us to hold negative beliefs. ("Homes are unaffordable. Prices are going to crash.") Then negative beliefs begin to screen out positive facts or information. Only the negative comes through. Seeing only the negative, we begin to hold our negative beliefs ever more tightly. They comfort us. Eventually, we see only what we have come to believe.

Negative Self-Talk Blocks Positive Fact-Finding

People who get caught up in this cycle of self-defeat cannot see their possibilities because they screen out facts that don't agree with these hopeless beliefs. Even worse, they close their minds to potential. To break this cycle, force yourself to consciously take note of each negative thought or belief that acts to cut you off from the future you want. Hook up an imaginary electrode to your mind. Give yourself a jolt every time you let negative thoughts short-circuit your problem-solving abilities. Whenever such thoughts occur, grab your mental channel selector. Switch to a different program. Every statement in the list of negative self-talk examples may contain an element of fact, a bit of truth. None reflects all the facts or the whole truth.

> **Every time a negative thought comes to you, zap it. Replace it with a positive thought. This takes energy, but the result will be stamina—positive stamina, a necessary ingredient for success.**

When you switch to clearer channels, you bring in a new picture, a picture that brings other facts and knowledge to your attention. More important, when you learn to switch channels and search for more positive pictures, you realize that you control your own destiny. You may not control the events and conditions of the world, but you do control how you respond to them.

Reprogram Your Self-Talk Tapes

How do you gain control and respond effectively? By reprogramming. First, erase all negative self-talk tapes that you keep replaying. Record over them with positive self-talk. When you erase your self-constructed limits, you replace them with possibilities. To illustrate: Closely think through the following questions. What are *your* possibilities? Don't worry if you can't answer all these questions now. You will be able to by the end of this book. But I do want you to get out of cruise control and start shifting into overdrive.

- What are six ways I can save more?
- What are six ways I can cut spending?
- What are six ways we can increase our income?
- What kinds of finance plans allow me to invest with little or nothing down?
- What are four ways we can overcome our credit problems?
- Who can serve as role models or mentors for us?
- Who do I know who can recommend a real estate agent who works with investors?
- What leading economic indicators are positive?
- What types of finance plans permit lower monthly payments?
- Where are the lower-priced up-and-coming cities and neighborhoods?
- Where and how might we find bargain-priced properties?
- What techniques are available to make investing easier?
- How can I persuade sellers to offer financing?
- Where can I find below-market interest rates?
- Who could I get to help us invest: parents, family, friends, investor, employer, co-owner, Donald Trump?
- What are 10 ways I could create value for this property or neighborhood?

All problem solving begins with questions. Yet it's only when you accept the idea of possibilities that you can come up with the questions to ask. Those who uncritically accept preprogrammed conclusions not only won't ask questions; they look past the choices that could solve their problems. That's why achieving wealth and financial freedom requires you to jolt yourself out of false, limiting beliefs. Once you erase these beliefs, your positive attitude alerts the mind to hunt down and lasso facts, knowledge, and experiences that lead to opportunity. Josh Billings, the celebrated nineteenth-century American humorist, used to joke, "I fear not the things I don't know, but rather the things I think I know that just ain't so."

As I said before, many tenants stuck in rentals believe they are blocked from home ownership. They believe they can't save, that they don't have adequate cash for a down payment, that they can't qualify for a mortgage, or that housing prices or monthly payments have climbed beyond their reach. They believe that nearly all their problems can be spelled M-O-N-E-Y. These hopeless renters underestimate their own potential. As a would-be investor, are you limiting your own progress with similar false beliefs?

As you read the following chapters, don't sell yourself short. Ask questions. Engage your mind. Make notes. Highlight ideas that can work for you. Reflect on your entrepreneurial possibilities. Review available choices. Create alternatives. If you want to build wealth with property, my years of real estate experience affirm you can. Your journey begins when you abandon negative, self-limiting beliefs. Through positive attitude and education, you can gain entrepreneurial altitude with a "can do—will do" list of possibilities.

DIG YOUR WELL BEFORE YOU'RE THIRSTY

No one makes it alone in real estate. You need a network of relationships with loan reps, real estate agents, title companies, property inspectors, lawyers, zoning/building regulators, handymen, contractors, and, of course, sellers, tenants, and, at some point, buyers.

When should you begin to meet these people, get to know them, and let them know you? Now! As Harvey McKay cleverly puts it, "Dig your well before you're thirsty."

Right now: Join your local real estate investment club. Go out and call on a variety of loan reps and loan brokers. Learn what kinds of deals they're doing. Learn what kinds of deals they want to do. Ask for names of dependable, competent, and reasonably priced service providers. It's never too early to build up your Rolodex (or Palm Pilot).

But remember, don't become a parasite—taking, never giving. Reciprocity is the name of the game. Ask how you can help the other party. People in real estate (and related services) appreciate referrals. When you know someone who's about to buy, sell, borrow, or renovate, give him or her the name of a service provider with whom you would like to grow a relationship. In tandem, tell that service provider that you referred someone to him or her and that he or she might even initiate contact with the person you know (with his or her permission, of course).

I once referred an investor friend to a real estate broker I had previously done business with in Dallas. I didn't think much more about it until six months later, when I opened my mail to find a thank-you note from the broker and a check for $10,000. It seems my friend (whom I had not recently talked with) had just closed on a $2.7 million neighborhood shopping center. Now that's reciprocity. To build and nurture relationships, live those three very big words: quid pro quo.

CURTAIL YOUR DESTRUCTIVE SPENDING AND BORROWING

The late night real estate infomercials entice with grand displays of luxury. They know their customers, and it's not (primarily) entrepreneurs. Infomercial customers consist of that large sector of the population who spend and borrow beyond their means. Why else emphasize the "no cash, no credit" sales pitch?

If you were to believe this sales pitch, you might conclude that real estate can quickly lift you from indebted spendthrift to a multimillionaire without extracting sacrifice and financial discipline. All gain, no pain.

Entrepreneurs know differently. To achieve wealth and financial freedom, ration your spending and eliminate destructive debt. If you earn $60,000 a year, live on $40,000 (or less). If you earn $100,000, live on $60,000 (or less). Never borrow to finance new cars, clothes, jewelry, travel, entertainment, or other affectations of the "good life." Only use your credit cards for convenience. Never use them to borrow money to finance what you otherwise can't afford.

The larger your discretionary income and the less your destructive debt (debt that finances a depreciating asset or lifestyle pleasure), the faster you can build your wealth and financial freedom. Read *The Millionaire Next Door* by Thomas Stanley. You will see that the great majority of self-made millionaires strictly curtail their personal spending and borrowing. More important, not one "Professor Stanley" we studied borrowed or spent lavishly during the early years of their serious wealth building.

Want to impress your bankers or property sellers? Do it with your strong credit score and financial statement, not a new Mercedes, a prestigious address, a Rolex watch, or an Armani suit. For wealth-building entrepreneurs, conspicuous consumption hurts much more than it helps. It slices away your power to invest and borrow constructively. It reinforces your "big hat, no cattle" reputation.

Plan Your Time, Shape Your Life

If you have time to be petty, it indicates you're not busy enough with your work.

Right now, list and describe your most important lifetime goals: health, fitness, wealth, freedom, love, charity? What else? How well does your actual time and effort invested (spent? wasted?) align with each of your goals?

If you're like most people, a yawning gap separates how you live from how you would like to live. Why? Because you fail to bring the future you want into the present. You spend too much time on small tasks and pleasures. You invest too little time mapping out the road to your hopes. As a result, weeks, months, and years pass by, and some of your most critical goals and priorities remain as distant as before.

Your Three "Budgets"

Everyone faces a mental budget, a money budget, and a time/ activity budget. Your mental budget refers to how well you allocate your thoughts, attitudes, and beliefs. Do you program your mind with negative self-talk, self-imposed limits, and puny aspirations? Or do you affirm and explore expansive ideas and creative possibilities? As to money, do you favor consumption over investment? Or do you discipline your current spending and destructive borrowing to ensure a prosperous future?

Ideally, up to this point, you've inventoried and reformed your dominating attitudes and beliefs. You've figured out how to allocate your finances more profitably. Now, inventory your hours. Surely, you've asked this question, "Where does the time go?" Now answer it.

Inventory the Use of Your Time (i.e., Life)

As a reader of this book, you rank wealth and financial freedom among your lifetime goals. Does the way you allocate your time reflect this goal? You will live 168 hours this week, next week, and each week thereafter. How many of those hours will you devote to looking at properties, building business relationships, reading related books and articles, and completing other activities that will move you closer to these goals?

I love people who get to the point when they call or come by. If they don't waste my time, I will take the time to talk with people.

To succeed as an entrepreneur, forget "wishing and hoping," forget "someday," forget "if I only had the time." Schedule the time. Squeeze out lower-priority, low-significance activities. Bring the future you want into view. What activities will you pursue today, this week, and in the weeks that follow that will help you banish "woulda, coulda, shoulda" from your self-talk? Want to change your life for the better? Change the way you live today.

HONOR YOUR APPOINTMENTS, PROMISES, AND AGREEMENTS

We encourage you to build productive, quid pro quo relationships. To obtain insightful information, referrals, and recommendations, provide others with information, referrals, and recommendations. But your successful career requires something more: dependability. When you agree to perform, perform as agreed.

Real estate attracts more than its share of fakes, pretenders, wannabes, sharks, shirkers, and weasels. In one way or another, all of these disreputable folks feel no need to honor their appointments, promises, and agreements. They show up late or not at all. They overpromise and underdeliver. They continue to push for concessions long after the deal is struck. They refuse to close contracts for slight or illegitimate reasons.

Although surprisingly some such folks hang around the business for years, their shortsighted one-upmanship costs them far more than they would gain through more respectable behavior.

At the start of my career, I expected sellers to finance my property investments. Yet as a middle-class college student, I lacked a bank credit record and possessed relatively little cash. Nevertheless, owners of rental properties soon began to call with unsolicited offers. I benefited from referrals because early on I established myself as a young, ambitious entrepreneur who followed through on my promises, contracts, and commitments.

The lesson: Distinguish yourself from the weasels, sharks, and pretenders. Establish your dependability. If your appointment is set for 9:00, show up at 8:55. If you shake hands on an agreement, don't try to extract a later concession without quid pro quo. If something changes and you must amend or default for good and unavoidable reasons, draft a revised plan of commitment that you can honor. Once you prove that others can count on you without worry or suspicion, I guarantee that good deals will seek you.

LEARN CONTINUOUSLY, IMPROVE CONTINUOUSLY

Every day brings change. Vacancy rates go up. Interest rates go down. Condo conversions fade. Lofts become popular. New types of financing appear. Revised zoning, tax, or landlord–tenant laws are enacted. Demographics, lifestyles, and cultural preferences never stand still.

For some would-be investors, change creates problems. For entrepreneurs, change alerts them to profitable opportunities.

Opportunity or Despair?

Say the year is 2002. You live in San Diego. Property prices have accelerated so fast that you can't locate reasonably priced properties in any of the neighborhoods where you would like to invest. What do you do? Complain? Tell yourself that you missed your chance for big profits? Indict yourself with "woulda, coulda, shoulda" recriminations? No, you would choose none of these responses.

As a possibility-driven entrepreneur, you would ask questions. You would explore other neighborhoods (National City?) and other cities (Las Vegas? Phoenix? Peoria?). You would investigate whether all types of San Diego properties had experienced the same fast rates of appreciation. You would evaluate the potential for converting apartments to condos. You would talk with members of southern California real estate investment clubs to learn where the smart money is flowing. You would buy and read books on foreclosures, fixer-uppers, condominiums, small-income properties, tax liens, and creative financing.

When most people see the door close to one opportunity, they give up. They resort to self-defeating self-talk. Entrepreneurs know that for every door that closes, another one opens.

Search for Possibilities

Case in point! During 2004 and 2005, I spoke on the programs at Robert Kyosaki's Los Angeles, San Jose, and San Francisco Rich Dad events. There, I talked with dozens of Californians who were actively looking for new investment ideas. They weren't depressed by high property prices or media babble about the bubble. These resourceful folks knew they could make money in real estate somehow, somewhere. Their job was to learn all they could and then act on that knowledge.

> **No one could make 40 Wall Street (now home to Trump University) work. They artificially limited their possibility thinking.**

Likewise, last month I spoke at a property show (seminars, exhibits) in London that featured Dubai, UAE villas and condos. That show attracted 2,300 visitors. Faced with sky-high London prices (and dismal weather), these intellectually curious attendees were not deterred from investing in real estate. They came to the London Dubai show with open minds and possibility thinking. They wanted to learn how they might profit in the world's fastest-growing sun-filled city ($25 billion under construction, $25 billion more in the planning and design stages).

You're On Your Way

You're reading this book. You clearly show a desire to learn. But don't stop here. Make learning a lifelong search for knowledge and improvement. Read, attend seminars and conferences, take short courses (such as those offered by Trump University), look at properties, and talk with people. Do not think that learning represents a discrete event. Seek to learn continuously wherever you are, whatever you're doing.

Everyone you know or meet has at one time or another bought, sold, rented, financed, remodeled, or invested in property. Learn from their experiences. Use that knowledge to generate ideas and improve your own performance.

We now turn to our eighth and perhaps most important entrepreneurial characteristic, how to make great decisions.

4

MAKE GREAT DECISIONS

"Too many people hire financial advisers and other experts," says Mr. Trump, "without realizing that those advisers can wreck their lives." Although Mr. Trump regularly consults with and relies on world class experts, such as golf course designer Tom Fazio and architects Helmut Jahn and I. M. Pei, he never abandons his responsibility to make the final decision after endless rounds of questions and research.

On one project, for example, Mr. Trump replaced Helmut Jahn because Mr. Trump decided that Jahn was not working well with the New York City planning staff. When it comes to market research, Mr. Trump makes the decisions. He doesn't employ a big staff of number crunchers to tell him where to build or what features to include. He gets to know his intended customers first hand.

I asked Jill Cremer, the Trump Organization's Vice President of Development and Marketing, what techniques the company uses to find locations to build. She laughed and said, "We ask Mr. Trump, that's our research." She went on to say that he also chose the carpeting, finishes, and other building exterior and interior details.

In one instance, when Mr. Trump completely delegated a major property management task, he regretted his lack of attention when trouble hit. "Unfortunately," he lamented, "I made a critical mistake. I should have gotten involved myself in the beginning."

Naturally, someone who runs a company the size of the Trump Organization can't do everything himself. But Mr. Trump is no Kenneth Lay. If something happens, Mr. Trump is there to take responsibility. "I want to get the opinions of others before I decide," says Mr. Trump, "but I've gained more knowledge by asking questions than I ever have by commissioning a consulting report."

Consult experts, but never abdicate. Ask questions of everyone and anyone. Frank McKinney, the iconic Florida builder of $50 million spec homes tells this anecdote about Mr. Trump. "When I first met Mr. Trump," says Frank, "he zipped right past the typical small talk. For the next 30 minutes straight, he fired questions at me to learn how I did so well in the luxury market. I've never met anybody so inquisitive."

> **Most people fear success; they fear commitment.
> They fear making decisions. That gives people like
> me who know how to make great decisions
> a formidable advantage.**

D O YOU ENDLESSLY MULL OVER "What should I do" types of
questions? Do you second-guess and rehash the decisions
you've made? Do you regret past decisions? Have your past decisions sometimes failed to produce the results you wanted? Would
you like to make better decisions in the future? If you answer yes
to any of these questions (and who wouldn't?), here's how to open
your life to a brighter future: Revise your decision-making *process* as
it applies to your investing and your life.

YOUR LIFE DEPENDS ON THE PROCESS YOU USE TO MAKE INVESTMENT DECISIONS

You can think positively, stifle your negative self-talk, plan your
schedule, make network connections, and learn everything about
everything. But to become a top-gun real estate entrepreneur, you
also have to figure out how to adjust your sights, where to aim, and
when to pull the trigger.

> **Sometimes we go on for hours in the boardroom to
> get all of the information we need to make
> a knowledgeable decision.**

In matters of real estate, as in matters of life, nothing sub-
stitutes for the ability to execute great decisions—decisions that
move you as quickly as possible toward where you need to go.
Unfortunately, few (if any) of the courses that schools and colleges offer provide much help. They're long on problem solving
but short on how to translate those "solutions" into profit-making
action.

Contrary to dogma, "knowledge isn't power" per se. To really power your life, you've got to put that knowledge to work. "I *knew* I should have . . ." doesn't get the job done. How do you increase the odds that your decisions will pay off the way you want them to? Easy. Do not focus on the decisions you need to make.

First, engineer a fail-safe decision-making system. Hundreds of times, I've heard people complain, "Man, I screwed that up. I really made a bad decision when I . . . " Yet rarely does anyone lament, "Gee, my decisions often turn out badly because I've got a lousy decision-making process." Nevertheless, more often than not, the fault does lie with the process.

So let's talk system. Let's work to improve the quality of your investment decision-making process. Here are five pointers that will help:

1. Rank priorities, explore possibilities.
2. Get your facts straight.
3. Use rules of thumb cautiously.
4. Question advice and recommendations (expert or otherwise).
5. Organize your thinking.

RANK PRIORITIES, EXPLORE POSSIBILITIES

"What *was I* thinking?" Surely you've asked yourself that question. Most often, this question pops into your mind when you realize that your decision seems to have come from left field. It bears little relation to favored priorities and possibilities. To avoid this lapse, get in touch with your feelings, values, and priorities. Think through multiple ways to reach your investment objectives.

Set Priorities

Know yourself. Know what you want. Know which goals and activities you would like to pursue. Rank your priorities in importance. Without ranked priorities to guide your decisions, either you drift without aim or your life reflects the chaos of a Marx Brothers comedy. You perpetually scurry in multiple directions—but never end up where you want to be.

Expand Your Possibilities

You may know where you want to go but not how to get there. Often people fail to make the decisions that best fit their goals and priorities because they narrowly limit their menu of choices. As I noted before, I met many renters at my Stop Renting Now! programs who truly valued home ownership but blocked themselves from this goal. They had not put forth the effort to learn their possibilities.

> **The reason I can move quickly is that I've done the background work first, which no one really notices.**

Likewise, I see eager sellers who dump their troubled properties. Yet other investors buy these "losers" and turn them into moneymakers. That's why savvy entrepreneurs need to persistently build up their stock of ideas and knowledge. When you command a diverse and extensive repertoire of possibilities, you will spot opportunity where others suffer defeat. In later chapters, you'll see scores of issues from which you can draw ideas to estimate and create value or, just as important, spot risk (danger). Naturally, you won't apply each one every time. But the full repertoire will definitely boost your power of possibility thinking: What can go right? What can go wrong? Great decisions anticipate both types of outcomes.

GET YOUR FACTS STRAIGHT

Quality decisions require accurate facts and data. Fortunately, such facts don't come easy. Why fortunately? Because when others fall for slipshod data and firehouse chatter, your thoughtful approach will give you a competitive advantage to deal with reality, not illusion. Before you accept a so-called fact, you will think, analyze, and verify.

When I started out, I spent a lot of time researching every detail pertinent to the deal. I still do the same today.

Say that someone tells you, "Vacancy rates in the area have jumped up to 9 percent. This isn't a good time to invest in rental properties." How should you interpret this information?

Facts vs. Opinion

To get your facts straight, distinguish *fact* from opinion. Opinions often masquerade as truth. Realize the difference. Even if the 9 percent vacancy figure is in some sense correct, the proscription that follows represents a view that may or may not hold merit. Beware! Much of the information you seek will be delivered to you as part fact (or maybe "fact"), part opinion. Clearly distinguish between the two.

At times, opinion even morphs into conventional wisdom, as with the so-called real estate bubble. The "bubble" opinion of property prices is just that: opinion. Yet most media commentators present it as fact. (As you will see in later chapters, pundits, many with ties to Wall Street, built the bubble theory on a sand beach without pilings of relevant facts and reasoning to support it.)

Nine Percent Vacancy: Fact, "Fact," or Fancy

I call a *fact* a data point that you can reasonably incorporate into your analysis and decisions. For example, you can generally obtain facts about interest rates, apartment rent levels, real estate listings, property sales prices, time on market, population growth, and the number of properties up for sale unsold (inventories).

What about vacancy rates? These figures more frequently reflect "fact" or fancy. By "fact," I mean a figure that displays some truth but that is of limited use in its raw form. When reported by market research and commercial/investment brokerage firms, vacancy rates usually fall into this iffy category—informative but in need of a closer look.

Before you rely on such a number, wisely ask questions such as the following:

- What geographic boundaries specifically delineate the area studied?
- How did the researchers gather their data? What sampling errors could distort the data?
- How does this 9 percent market vacancy rate differ among properties according to building size, unit mix, price ranges, amenities, features, condition, location, and so on? (Maybe one large 400-unit HUD Section 8–dominated property accounts for 40 percent of the vacancies in the total area under study. Maybe studio apartments enjoy waiting lists; three-bedroom, one-baths remain tough to fill.) When you speak of vacancy rates (as just one example), market segments and market niches matter greatly.
- Where are vacancy rates headed? Snapshots rarely provide a full, dynamic view. You need trend lines and reasoned forecasts that look to the future.

Sometimes "facts" are better characterized as fancy. For any number of reasons, the people you talk with (or read) may not know what they are talking about. Obviously, we all inadvertently make mistakes. On other occasions, sales agents (as do lawyers) give answers without facts so as not to appear ignorant. In some instances, people purposely mislead. Does that apartment manager really want to truthfully disclose to the market researcher that her building's rent roll turns over twice a year and that vacancies have climbed above 25 percent? I don't think so.

Think, Analyze, Verify

Savvy entrepreneurs search beyond conventional wisdom, "facts," opinions, and fanciful dodges or assertions. They know that quality facts provide the ingredients for quality decisions. As you move forward in real estate (and life), use multiple data points and sources of information. Before you interpret, think, analyze, and verify. Avoid a rush to judgment. The world overflows with GIGO (garbage in, garbage out) decision making. But with facts, you can outperform the conventional crowd.

Napoleon said, "A leader has the right to be beaten but never the right to be surprised." Know your customers!

USE RULES OF THUMB CAUTIOUSLY

Recently, I bought a property from an out-of-town owner. This owner really didn't want to sell, nor had he even placed his property on the market. Nevertheless, I persuaded him to consider my generous offer of $90 p.s.f. (dollars per square foot represents a rule-of-thumb measure of value).

Given that this owner had bought this property many years ago, my offer provided him a large windfall gain. He became interested. Still, because he lived out of town and lacked up-to-date information on local property prices, he told me that before signing a contract, he wanted to test my offer against the advice of a sales agent.

"No," the sales agent reported, "$90 p.s.f. is too low. The going price is around $100 p.s.f."

The seller called back and told me he would sell at $100 p.s.f. I complained, "That price is too high. The property needs a lot of work. You're taking advantage of me because you know I want the property."

Alas, my complaints and dickering fell on deaf ears. I gave in. "Okay," I responded, "against my better judgment, I guess I can go to $100 p.s.f. You just got my top dollar."

The Appraisal

"Holy cow!" the mortgage loan appraiser said to me as I showed him around the property. "Given the price you paid, I thought this place would be wrecked. I'm going to report a figure at the low end of the value range for this property, but that's still 20 percent more than your contract price. How did you find such a steal?"

The Owner/Agent's Error

When the sales agent gave the seller her rule-of-thumb valuation of $100 p.s.f., she recited a "fact," not a *fact*. True, on average, properties in the area had sold for the price she quoted. But the owner should not have relied on that rule-of-thumb figure for two reasons:

1. *Out of Date:* At the time, properties in that market were appreciating quickly. The rule-of-thumb figure of $100 p.s.f. reflected past closed sales, not pending contracts. More recently, current buyers had bid prices up another 10 to 15 percent.
2. *Unique Features:* As a second factor, this subject property differed favorably from the average. Units displayed open floor plans, garden views, and bright/light interiors (because of skylights and many large windows.) The units were also smaller than average. (All things being equal, smaller units tend to sell for higher p.s.f. prices than larger ones.)

Never Base Your Decisions on a Rule of Thumb

In real estate, you will run across many rules of thumb (discussed in later chapters). Such common indicators apply to measures such as gross rent multipliers, capitalization rates, price p.s.f.s, construction costs, energy costs, remodeling costs, maintenance expense ratios, rental rates, vacancy rates, and so on. Never accept such rules of thumb as *fact*.

Investigate further. Each market, every property, displays unique features and conditions. Before you apply any facts or rules of thumb, verify their specific relevance to your property or problem. (Of course, when you negotiate to buy or sell, use rules of thumb that favor your position to persuade the other party that your offer is reasonable and justified.)

QUESTION ADVICE AND RECOMMENDATIONS
(EXPERT AND OTHERWISE)

Real estate gurus tell you to establish a team of individuals to whom you can turn for advice and recommendations. In our complex world, no one person can know everything. Good advice.

I go over every detail with my experts. They're on my team, but I'm the General.

Yet heed this warning: Never abdicate critical decisions to your advisers—regardless of whether they're trusted friends and family or world-class experts. Recall the out-of-town owner from whom I bought a property. He carelessly relied on his expert real estate agent. In doing so, he gave up $130,000 of potential profit.

The people you turn to for advice can fail you for a variety of reasons, some benign, some not so. Either way, your decision (and bank account) suffers. When dealing with investment advisers, guard against these five pitfalls:

- Advice or approval?
- Knowledge or ignorance?
- Your preferences or theirs?
- Conflict of interest?
- Public soothsayers or media molls?

Advice or Approval?

Ask yourself, "Do I really want critical counsel?" We all know people who ask for advice but really want approval. In response, we approve. Why start an argument? The advisee then uses the approval to further justify what he wanted to do all along.

To gain most from advice, make sure you seek "no holds barred" counsel. Then listen, weigh, interpret, and apply as you deem wise. If you do not really want additional perspective, insight, or critique, don't burden your advisers with pretense. Don't seek advice for the same reason that a drunk seeks a lamppost—support, not illumination.

If undiluted support for your preconceived ideas is what you want, your friends, family, or consultants will probably oblige. But when that's the case, recognize this advice for what it is—"go along to get along," not disinterested critique.

Knowledge or Ignorance?

Do those you ask for advice possess the information, experience, and expertise necessary to advise you intelligently? Unless your friends or relatives have recently been shopping for property in the same city and neighborhood where you've been looking, they can't tell you whether you're getting a good buy. If your lawyer sister hasn't seen a real estate contract since her Real Property 101 course in law school, chances are she's not the one who should review your purchase agreement.

You may work with one of the best and brightest real estate agents in town, but if your property search takes you into neighborhoods or communities where your agent can't find her way without studying a map, it's time to bring in an agent who's more familiar with the area. Whether friend, relative, lawyer, or sales agent, just because someone offers an opinion does not mean he or she actually knows enough about your problem and goals to provide the counsel you need.

General Rule or Exception

Several years ago, I consulted a certified public accountant (CPA) to complete my federal income tax returns. During the years in question, I had served as a visiting professor at the University of

Illinois, 1,000 miles distant from my permanent home in Florida. I told this tax professional that I wanted to deduct the living expenses I incurred while working in Champaign–Urbana.

"No, you can't do that," he emphatically declared. "Regardless of where you own a house, your tax home is located where your job is located."

Fortunately, I knew the law better than this tax specialist. As a general tax rule, the CPA stood correct. He erred with his advice because tax law specifically states that employees may deduct their job-related living expenses when working temporarily away from home. (We need not go into the technical issue here.)

My point is that experts may know general rules and practices very well. But every subject, from accounting to zoning, involves many specialized details. You may, for example, assume that conversations with your lawyer are private and privileged. As a general rule, you're right. Sue your lawyer for malpractice, and you'll be rudely surprised. That lawsuit voids the lawyer's previously inviolable pledge of confidentiality.

When you seek advice and recommendations, verify that your counselor actually knows the exceptions as well as the general rules. Had I followed that CPA's advice instead of the *exceptional* temporary work rule, my tax bill would have increased $8,000. Beware of generalists when you need a specialist.

Up to Date?

On one occasion when I solicited legal advice on a property transaction, the lawyer informed me of the relevant law. On the basis of his analysis, I proceeded through the transaction. All too late, I learned that the lawyer had erred. The law in question had actually changed six months prior to the date I sought advice. The lawyer had failed to stay current. His error cost me more than $100,000. (Malpractice? I'll save that story for another time.)

When dealing with experts, do not assume that their advice reflects the latest developments. Question the date of their data, information, and knowledge. As with milk and eggs, the use-by date for advice may have expired.

Age of Discontinuities

Real estate investors frequently look at past trend lines before they buy, renovate, or sell a property. They want to learn where the market *has been* moving. The real question, though, becomes more difficult to answer: Will current trends continue, or will discontinuities intervene? Here's an example.

Throughout the 1990s, single-family houses appreciated faster than condominiums. In many cities, condominiums barely appreciated at all. Because of this poor performance, by 2001 nearly all supposed experts in real estate provided this advice: "If you want a good investment, don't buy a condo. Choose a condo only for lifestyle and affordability. Condominiums make lousy investments."

I differed from this prevailing negative forecast for condominiums. I believed that the slow-growth condo price trend of the past decade would not repeat itself. To explain my reasoning, in 2002, I wrote a book, *Make Money with Condominiums and Townhouses*.

In that book, I urged property investors (and home buyers) to ignore the past and look to the future. Market conditions had changed in the following eight ways:

1. *Demographics I:* An increasing number of baby boomers were becoming empty nesters. They no longer wanted the big house and its time and expense of upkeep.
2. *Demographics II:* As of the early 2000s, the echo boomers were coming of age. Condos appeal not only to their empty-nester parents but also to younger people who are buying their first home.
3. *Urban Living:* Throughout the 1990s, many cities reduced crime, revitalized downtown areas, and in general made city living more appealing. In addition, traffic congestion stuck commuters in intolerable delays. In-town condo living permitted escape from traffic hassles.

4. *Price Differences:* When one type (or location) of property appreciates faster than another, sooner or later many would-be buyers switch their preferences to the lower-priced alternatives.

5. *Lock and Leave:* People today travel more for both business and pleasure. They increasingly like the lock-and-leave lifestyle that condominiums make possible.

6. *Second (and Third) Homes:* Beginning in the late 1990s, demand for second homes grew substantially. (See my book, *How to Buy Second Homes for Vacation, Retirement, and Investment*). As often as not, second home buyers choose condos and townhouses.

7. *Rent vs. Own:* The low interest rates of the early 2000s changed the rent–buy equation. With mortgage rates at 6 percent or less, tenants who preferred apartment living began to realize that they could own their own apartment for less than they were paying in rent.

8. *Investor Demand:* After stocks crashed in 2000, millions of investors began looking for good investment alternatives. Even without appreciation, condos in many areas yielded great returns just from cash flows and mortgage payoff (amortization of the loan).

In addition to these eight reasons, my close study of the then current market (2000–2002) revealed that condo sales had picked up, prices had begun to increase, time on market for listings was falling, and condo/townhouse "for sale" inventories were shrinking. While most expert comments were stuck in the past, my emphasis on the latest facts and market conditions (demand and supply) convinced me that conventional wisdom erred. Condos and townhouses would soon generously reward their investors.

Was I right? Yes. "Condo Price Increases Again Outpace Houses," headlined a recent article in *The New York Times*. In my Florida hometown, condos and townhouses that sold for $125,000 in 2000 now quickly sell at $250,000.

Will condo owners enjoy similar profits over the next five or six years? In general, I don't think so. Again, market conditions have changed. First, the rent–buy equation does not look as favorable today. Second, investor cash flows have fallen because condo prices have jumped up faster than rents. Third, builders and condo converters are bringing (nationwide) hundreds of thousands of additional condominiums into the market.

By pointing out these changes in market conditions, I am not saying that you can no longer expect to make money with condominiums and townhouses. In fact, I am still looking to buy. I believe that well-selected condos and townhouses will outperform stocks, bonds, and many single-family houses.

I am saying, however, that this condo example illustrates the importance of discontinuities—both in looking forward from today as well as when I looked forward from the early 2000s. Before you accept an expert's trend line forecast into the years ahead, satisfy yourself that no changes lurk to shatter that crystal ball. Facts change, trends reverse.

Your Preferences or Theirs?

Do your advisers truly understand your needs and goals? Or are they really advising you to judge the world as they do? When we ask for advice, we often do not fully explain our needs, goals, or the most important things we're trying to achieve. Sometimes we don't even know ourselves. Likewise, when we offer counsel, we tend to shade recommendations toward our own biases. We don't focus on the other person's perspective.

If you ask your brother to tell you what he thinks of that fixer-upper, three-bedroom ranch in Windsor Heights, he could answer, "No way! I wouldn't even think about buying that dog of a property." Has your brother answered according to your needs? Or does he have some personal bias against fixer-uppers or Windsor Heights? What if a real estate agent tells you Troy Woods is not a good area?

Should you accept that advice without inquiry? Or should you ask why the agent holds that view? Maybe this agent doesn't like Troy Woods because he doesn't think much of its public schools.

What Does Your Target Market Want?

Yet if your target market of renters or buyers does not live in families with children, perhaps schools won't matter much to them. Alternatively, maybe the neighborhood includes a nearby, reasonably priced private school. Or maybe the poor-school issue has so beaten down property prices in that district that the neighborhood now fits your investment strategy: Find relatively low-priced areas that offer strong promise for turnaround. As an ambitious neighborhood entrepreneur, you might spearhead a campaign for community revitalization and school improvement.

Sometimes advisers parrot approval of your ideas as a "go along to get along" tactic. More often, they paint their advice with colors that match their own picture of the world. Before you ask for advice or recommendations, clearly explain the goals that you want your decision to accomplish.

Personal Reflection

Here's another personal reflection on this point: Dozens of times each year, I meet people who take a minute or so to describe a property to me. Then they ask, "What do you think? Does it sound like a good investment?"

I like to help aspiring investors whenever I can. But with such rapid-fire data dumps, I cannot provide useful input about the merits of the property.

A quick recitation of facts (or maybe "facts") hardly fixes a solid base on which to hang my recommendation. Second, no property represents a "good" investment apart from the risks, rewards, and goals that remain personal to the investor. Rather than respond something like, "Yeah, seems like a good deal. I'd encourage you to go for it" (which I suspect most want me to say), I answer, "What are your goals, talents, inclinations, and plans? Have you performed your due diligence? How do your answers to these questions match up together?"

Do not abdicate your decisions to experts—me or anyone else. Even if I am convinced that your deal looks great in the abstract, it still might not work as the right deal for you.

That's why I qualify the universal advice that tells investors to "deal only with motivated sellers." Regardless of its potential to yield profits, this technique does not match the strategies and goals that most people prefer to adopt. As a result, most who try it soon abandon the approach in disappointment.

Conflict of Interest?

Do your advisers' interests conflict with yours? When you rely on the advice of other people, detail how their interests may conflict with yours. Some unethical real estate agents may try to talk you into a property or mortgage finance plan that doesn't meet your needs just so they can gain a commission or kickback. Your friends or parents may talk against an outlying neighborhood because they'd rather see you live closer to them. Your friends could advise you not to invest in real estate because they're jealous, or maybe they think that you will drift apart as friends as you pursue new activities and responsibilities.

People have their own reasons for the advice they offer. They may want to help you make a better decision. They may be pursuing their own agenda. When someone says, "This is what you ought to do," take a moment to reflect. Think through the knowledge, perspectives, and *motives* that prompt such advice.

Don't Believe Everything You Read

Have you ever wondered why the personal finance magazines heavily promote the idea, "Over the long run stocks (will) have outperformed all other investments?" Because it's true? Hardly. Rather, take a look at the magazine's advertisers—mutual funds, stockbrokers, and life insurers who sell stock-based retirement and investment plans.

In like manner, few local newspapers run articles that criticize real estate brokers (or automobile dealers). These two businesses alone often account for more than 30 percent of newspaper advertising revenues.

Public Soothsayers or Media Molls?

Too many schooled professionals believe themselves experts even though they have never demonstrated any competence in the areas in which they routinely offer advice to the public. Indeed, the media promote this misplaced conceit.

I never accept anything I read or hear from brokers, sellers, buyers, tenants, experts, television. I want to dig in and verify the facts.

Economic Forecasts Rarely Forecast Correctly

Newspapers, magazines, and cable news, for example, refer to their quoted economic forecasters as experts. But for the most part, the expertise (if any) of these commentators lies in their intricate knowledge of theoretical economic models. Few, if any, consistently render accurate forecasts. Most famously, perhaps, in the field of real estate, Harvard economist Gregory Mankiw (later to become chairman of President George W. Bush's Council of Economic Advisers), in a 1989 research article, predicted a collapse in housing prices. He forecasted that between 1989 and 2005, home prices would steadily fall by 40 percent. Rather than fall, most properties during that period doubled or tripled in value.

When Alan Greenspan appeared before Congress to testify about his competency to become chairman of the Federal Reserve, a senator asked, "Mr. Greenspan, we have reviewed your forecasts about the U.S. economy during the past decade. It seems that your predictions have erred far more often than they have proved correct."

Greenspan responded, "Yes sir, my forecasts often have missed the mark. I can say, though, that fortunately, other aspects of my career have achieved higher rate of success."

Financial Planners: Technocratic Expertise or Investment Savvy?

Although few financial planners display out-of-the-ordinary investment savvy, the press promotes them as financial experts and routinely quotes their investment recommendations and asset allocations. Such expertise remains questionable. In the late 1990s, I never read one quoted financial planner who advised investors to sell stocks and buy property.

Quite the opposite. Then and now, most *quoted* financial planners claim, "If you own your own home, you've got all of the exposure to real estate you need. Over the long run, count on stocks to outperform all other asset classes."

Financial planners should know the technical rules of tax-deferred retirement planning, the investment styles of various mutual funds, and the source of low-cost annuities. They certainly know the conventional wisdom of investing and asset allocation as propagated by the theoretical finance professors. But few practicing financial planners (as opposed to media molls) even claim to know how to beat the market.

Moreover, the certified financial planner course work devotes only three hours to the topic of real estate investing—the world's largest asset class. Contrary to media boosts, financial planners per se do not excel as investors any more than economists excel as forecasters.

Uncharitable Critique

In stating this less-than-charitable critique of economists, financial planners, and other experts who serve as media molls, I do not

intend wholesale indictment. Most such professionals define themselves as technocrats, not soothsayers. They competently deal with
the technical and theoretical issues of economics, investment selection, and portfolio diversification. I place on trial only those investment commentators (often economists and financial planners, but
they are not the only members of this species) who publicly advise
investors about swings in interest rates, the direction of housing
prices, which stocks to pick, currency exchange rates, and other
similar topics on which these experts have shown no superior fore-
casting skills.

Experience proves that media experts err with their investment
forecasts and opinions more often than they get things right. Never
base your investment decisions on such advice—even when it represents so-called expert consensus. For instance, in January 2005,
based on currency exchange rates, expert consensus forecasted a
huge 12-month fall of the dollar against the euro. By the end of
December 2005, the dollar had risen 10 to 15 percent against the
euro (January 2005: €1 = \$1.35; December 2005: €1 = \$1.18).

Advice and Counsel Redux

Early in my career, I erred egregiously because I wrongly assumed
that my lawyer held expertise in areas (negotiation and litigation)
when he clearly did not. That experience and others have repeatedly taught me not to abdicate my investment decisions to experts
and advisers.

Learn from my experience. Never assume that your lawyer, CPA,
real estate agent, mortgage broker, financial planner, medical doctor,
dentist, or other reputed expert knows enough to advise you in all
the areas for which you seek advice. Be wary of media commentators
who show little or no record of success in the areas where they offer
advice. Question, probe, and explore issues. Then, only if you're satisfied with an expert's verified counsel should you incorporate that
advice into your decision making.

You can't wear a blindfold in business.

Develop Your Ability to Question

I hear you object: "But, I don't know anything about. . . . How can I ask my experts pointed, intelligent questions? How can I explore issues when I don't even know the relevant issues?"

You can develop this skill to question and probe through practice and education. How many laypeople know anything about cancer, heart problems, or other illnesses? Nevertheless, they are learning. Throughout the United States, an increasing number of patients no longer accept without question the diagnoses and prescriptions of the medical establishment.

Medical specialists told *Saturday Evening Post* editor James Cousins that he needed to get his personal and business affairs in order, as he had six months to live. Modern medicine offered no hope. Cousins refused to accept this death sentence. He studied his illness. He explored alternatives that lay outside the diagnostic and prescriptive models of medical conventions. He developed his own treatment plan. He lived another 10 years. (Cousins tells his story in his book *Anatomy of an Illness*.)

Sometimes experts know the answers we're seeking. Sometimes they don't. Because of this fact, savvy entrepreneurs (as do savvy medical patients) learn to probe, question, and challenge their experts *before* they make a decision on the basis of such advice or recommendations.

Put It in Writing

When you choose to rely on personal professional advice, put it in writing. During your conversations, take detailed notes. In follow-up, write the adviser (lawyer, accountant, appraiser, consultant, real estate agent, loan rep, contractor, and so on) a thank-you letter. In that correspondence, set a tone of appreciation for his or her helpful advice. Accent the adviser's expertise, restate your understanding of the issues, and discuss what decision you plan to make that flows from the information the adviser provided.

This letter achieves three purposes: (1) It helps build your relationship (everyone likes a letter of appreciation), (2) it gives the adviser a chance to correct errors on his or her part or misinterpretations from your end, and (3) if the counsel subsequently proves faulty, your written note confirms the substance of the advice. Such evidence promotes peaceful remedy or, if necessary, supports a claim through lawsuit or regulatory complaint.

When you place advice in writing, you not only reduce the chance of error but also increase the chance of a satisfactory informal settlement or legal recovery. With written evidence, you avoid "I said, you said" quarrels that rarely produce the results you prefer.

ORGANIZE YOUR THINKING

To make decisions in real estate, you will sort through *facts* about property features, zoning laws, building regulations, target markets, vacancy rates, new construction, contracts, promotion, financing, economic conditions, and thousands of other details. This task raises two questions: How can you possible make sense out of all this information? How can you even know what information you need to collect?

> **If you can't organize your thoughts quickly and come to a decision, that good deal you were looking at will have been snapped up by someone else.**

In the following pages of this book, we answer these two questions. Just as aircraft pilots rely on a preflight checklist to prepare for takeoff, you need a takeoff plan to guide your real estate entrepreneuring. Instead of a checklist, however, we'll call this takeoff guide, the DUST framework. This entrepreneurial flight plan spells out the details to consider when you decide whether to buy and, if so, how much to pay for properties (or other opportunities, such as options, leases, air rights, or mortgages). Just as important, DUST shows you how to create the right marketing strategy and tactics to add value for your tenants, your buyers, and yourself.

Thus far, in Chapters 3 and 4, you have learned a good set of questions and guidelines to refine and advance the process you employ to make investment decisions. In the pages that follow, you're going to discover how to ask questions, collect facts, identify possibilities, and reason through your decisions to estimate, forecast, and create property values. To achieve your goals, you need both a systematic and thorough thinking process and an entrepreneurial guide to recognize and realize opportunities to create value for others and yourself.

Winners see problems as a great way to prove themselves.

5

SHARPEN YOUR ENTREPRENEURIAL THINKING

Organize your information for quick retrieval and thorough understanding.

EVER SINCE WILLIAM NICKERSON WROTE his now classic *How I Turned $1,000 into a Million in My Spare Time* (1959), best-selling real estate authors have been revealing "the secrets of my success." "Just follow these six steps," they say. "I'll give you everything you need to know." Sounds easy.

But here's the catch: If you adopt an investment approach that was developed by someone else in another place and time, you may end up losing your bank account. And, most certainly, you will miss the best opportunities that actually present themselves to you (albeit often unannounced). Why? Because real estate markets experience continuous change.

PROBLEMS OR OPPORTUNITIES?

Nothing remains the same: interest rates; vacancy rates; property prices; rent levels; employment; population demographics; consumer tastes, preferences, attitudes, and lifestyles; the cost and supply of new construction; government zoning rules, regulations, and restrictions. Every change creates problems and opportunities.

Fuse knowledge with imagination. In no time, you'll create something great to put in your "think big" tank.

That's why the same business plan that flooded you with profits last year could run dry next year. Just look at the big-name companies (such as IBM, Polaroid, Kodak, AT&T, Delta Airlines, General Motors, Conseco, Kmart) that once excelled with their well-crafted business models but subsequently suffered near-fatal losses because they failed to revise their entrepreneurial strategies in response to changes such as technology, competition, consumer preferences, and emerging lifestyles.

It All Depends

No one can tell you the easy way to real estate riches. It's natural for people to believe that someone else can tell them exactly what they need to do to make a fortune in real estate. Most of us shun ambiguity. But real estate's not that simple. Yes, learn from the experiences of others. You can certainly get ideas that you may want to try. Serious real estate investors read everything they can find that might lead to improved performance.

Setbacks are a part of life. Don't let them knock you off your feet.

Nevertheless, before you jump to follow a well-publicized investment technique or real estate guru, remember that the best answer to "Will it work?" remains, "It all depends."

A Strategy of Your Own

In this book, I won't mislead you with "five magic paths" or "seven easy steps" to real estate riches. I won't pretend that you can profitably buy, improve, and manage properties without some investment of effort, time, intelligence, and at least a workable amount of seed capital.[1]

However, I do promise to provide the knowledge and techniques necessary for you to develop a profitable, wealth-building strategy of your own. In the real world, you will conquer the challenges and vicissitudes of property markets only when you know how to discover and adapt as problems arise and opportunities unfold. In other words, from this book—as with no other—you will learn to think like an entrepreneur.

---

[1] This money does not necessarily have to come from your pocket. Partners or relatives quite frequently provide seed capital and credit for both beginning and experienced real estate investors.

MVP: The One Constant Rule

To think like an entrepreneur, you adopt one central rule: I call this unifying rule (or principle) the MVP (most valued property). When tenants (or buyers) search for a place to live or operate their business, they compare features, amenities, location, rent levels, lease terms, and dozens of other details that add to (or detract from) the usefulness of the property. They compare, contrast, weigh, and consider. In the end, which property do they eventually choose? The cheapest? Not necessarily. The best? Probably not. The biggest? Perhaps, but don't count the money just yet.

Create you business plan before you buy. You want to have Plan A, Plan B, and Plan C for adding value to the property.

At the moment of truth, tenants (buyers) will choose the property that offers the best value relative to all the other properties that they have considered. Hence, your entrepreneurial thinking should guide you to provide the MVP for your intended customers. From your perspective, MVP also means the property designs, features, and use that will add the most value to your net worth (i.e., the most valuable property). In other words, the MVP principle urges you to give your target customers their best value, while also maximizing the economic value of the property to you.

Few Owners Achieve MVP

During the past 20 years, I probably have looked at 5,000 (for-rent, for-sale) properties throughout the world (the United States, Canada, Mexico, Europe, Asia, the Middle East, and Australia). At least 90 percent of these properties fell short of MVP status for customers or investors.

The property's owner, manager, or sales agent had never thought systematically about the question of MVP: "How can we enhance our total value proposition in ways that would better satisfy (wow) our customers (tenants, buyers) and at the same time pull more dollars through to our bottom line?"

Every building that carries my name promises the highest quality available.

Make MVP Your Goal

To improve in any area of life, you must want to improve. You must make the effort. You must believe that the effort will pay off. You reprogram your mental tapes with positive self-talk and possibility thinking. In sum, you develop an entrepreneurial attitude (which will elevate your altitude). So now, let's review the DUST guide to your entrepreneurial flight plan.

THE DUST ENTREPRENEURIAL FRAMEWORK

An Overview

I'm really not a tough guy. But when it comes to education and using your brains, ignorance can be very expensive.

Study Figure 5.1 from top to bottom. Focus on how this framework guides your strategic reasoning process. You create an MVP when you shape your property toward demand and away from supply. Then develop the transfer (promotion and contracts) process necessary to lease or sell at the greatest profit. DUST[2] addresses your six decision points:

---

[2] The acronym DUST refers to four key areas that savvy entrepreneurs investigate: (1) Demand, (2) Utility, (3) Supply, and (4) Transfer process.

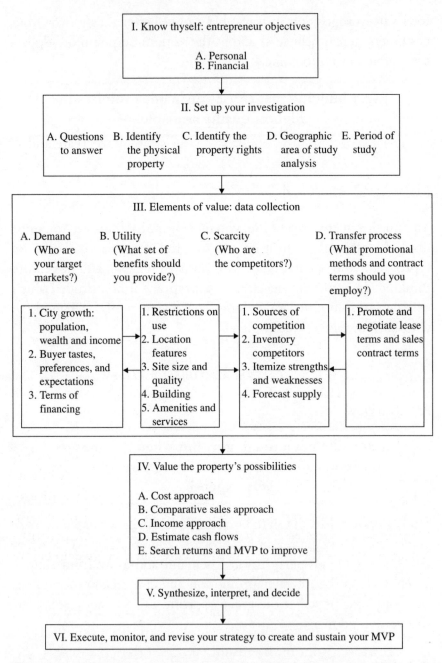

Figure 5.1 DUST Entrepreneurial Decision Framework for Creating Wealth through Real Estate. Copyright © Gary W. Eldred. Reprinted with permission.

I. Entrepreneurial objectives: Know thyself.
II. Set up your property, market study, and investment analysis.
III. Collect property and market data.
IV. Value the property possibilities from the perspective of customers and your financial goals.
V. Synthesize, interpret, and decide.
VI. Execute, monitor, and revise your strategy to create and sustain the property's MVP status.

ENTREPRENEURIAL OBJECTIVES: KNOW THYSELF

Who are you? What goals do you want to achieve? Take stock of your personal and financial resources, your talents, and your risk tolerance. Then choose an investment program and market strategy that will serve your purposes and desired style of life. Let your priorities and values guide your decision process. "I want to make a lot of money" may reflect your base desire. But to make that goal come true, align your efforts, feelings, and resources. Otherwise, you could walk a path that fails to lead to your destination.

Talents, Inclinations, Resources, Priorities

When I began buying and renovating properties, I not only lacked a clear entrepreneurial plan but also failed to inventory my talents and inclinations. Only after trial and error did I manage to create an investment program that worked personally and financially. Many would-be real estate entrepreneurs choose the wrong investment program or the wrong way to execute and then give up before they've achieved their full potential.

Assess your interests. What do you love? Create a blueprint for your life. Without goals, no momentum. Without momentum, your just daydreaming.

Become proactive. Design your investing to align with your personal values, abilities, resources, likes, dislikes, and priorities.

"No pain, no gain" still rules. Don't fool yourself into believing in the perfect match. As you deliberate choices, envision the life of freedom and financial security you want. To make it a reality, sacrifice and trade-offs are part of the bargain.

1. *Time and Money:* How many hours per week or per month are you willing to invest? What does your financial profile look like (credit, cash, earnings, borrowing power)?
2. *Trade Skills:* What types of handyman talents do you possess? Do you enjoy this type of work?
3. *Creativity and Design:* Do you enjoy searching out new ideas? Are you willing to learn and adapt the ideas of other? Would you like looking at properties, attending trade shows, and browsing through magazines and journals on property management, creative improvements, and related topics?
4. *Partners:* Do you prefer to play as a one-man band? Or would you like to join with others to share equity financing, work, responsibilities, and decision making?
5. *Tenants:* What types of people would you like to attract as tenants?
6. *Real Estate Agents:* Do you want to search and sell on your own? Or will you enlist the help of real estate agents?
7. *Numbers:* Can you learn to work with income statements, cash flows, rate-of-return calculations, cost estimates, budgets, and tight rehab and renovation budgets and schedules?
8. *Personal Achievement:* What types of real estate would give you the greatest sense of personal achievement and pride of accomplishment?

To succeed as a real estate entrepreneur, anticipate and prepare. Match your expectations to reality. Some property owners try to "do it all." They burn out. Others buy with "little or nothing down" and then find they lack the cash or credit necessary to handle repairs or cover losses from vacancies or bad debts. (Such investors or home owners, though, often create distressed sellers who sell at bargain prices—"just to get rid of this headache." Their problem becomes your opportunity.)

**Passion conquers fear. Take a tip from Nike—
"Just do it."**

Review Your Spending and Borrowing

The promoters of nothing-down real estate have pulled too many starry-eyed investor wannabes down the path to financial ruin with their mantra of "no cash, no credit, no problem." While it's certainly true that you can buy real estate without cash or credit, that fact begs the question. If that's your situation, why don't you have any cash or credit?

Please, exercise financial discipline and responsibility. "No cash, no credit" certainly poses a problem for those whose empty wallets result from destructive spending and borrowing. Many authors (including myself) have extensively written on this topic elsewhere. We need not go over the same territory here. But realize that investing in real estate will best put you on the road to financial freedom when you borrow constructively and spend miserly.[3]

Review your credit capacity, available cash, and monthly cash flow. How much money can you allocate to real estate acquisitions and fix-up work while you still maintain a reserve to cover contingencies and emergencies? Because you run some chance of mistake, stay within your limits. Use your first properties to gain experience and fine-tune your abilities and strategy.

What is your credit score? In their efforts to determine whether you're a good credit risk, mortgage lenders (and many owner-will-carry sellers) will check your credit score. Although a variety of credit-scoring systems exist, among the most widely used

---

[3] Again, I'll mention the insightful book that describes the personal discipline necessary to become wealthy; see *The Millionaire Next Door* by Thomas Stanley.

scores are those calculated by the Fair Isaac Corporation (FICO). To learn your FICO scores, go to www.myfico.com. For around $35, Fair Isaacs will provide three scores (as calculated from your credit data on file with Experian, TransUnion, and Equifax), suggest ways you can improve them, and let you know how your scores compare to the general population. On the basis of your credit profile, FICO estimates the interest rate that lenders will charge you. (The higher your credit score, the lower your interest rate and vice versa.)

What is your net worth? Your financial net worth consists of the total value of what you own less the total amount you owe to others. (If you've previously completed a mortgage application, you're probably familiar with this form, which is called a personal balance sheet.)

How liquid are you? Mortgage lenders will scrutinize your assets and net worth, but they also will evaluate your cash position. The more cash in your accounts, the easier you can weather setbacks. You (or your partners) will also need cash to close (down payment, closing costs, property repairs, and perhaps property improvements). If your balance sheet shows little cash (including near cash such as stocks, bonds, or certificate of deposits), sell some assets (cars, boats, vacation home, jewelry, and so on) to beef up your cash account. Liquidity not only adds to your borrowing power but also gives you the ready money to quickly jump on good deals when you spot them.

How much free cash flow do you generate each month? Some people spend and borrow so heavily that there's little if any money left at the end of the month. Living payday to payday stifles your ability to build wealth.

Boost your free cash flow. What spending you can slash? What debts you can eliminate? What luxuries (frivolities) you can do without? As financial planners emphasize, to build wealth while you're still young enough to enjoy it, curtail your destructive spending and borrowing. Live well *below* your means. Dollars you invest today can easily pay back 10 times over within a decade (or less).

Financial Goals

Okay, you've reviewed your financial wherewithal and personal preferences. It's time for goal setting. How much wealth would you like to create during the next 5, 10, or 20 years? How many properties would you like to acquire? In what price range? Do you plan to fix and flip, fix and hold, or passively buy and hold? Write out the numbers. Explore possibilities. Think big. Once you've settled on a goal, draft a business plan. Attach a timetable. Set deadlines. Without a written business plan, timetable, and goals, you will likely procrastinate. You will drift. You will lapse into "woulda, coulda, shoulda." Avoid this perpetual trap. Commit yourself with a business plan and specific action steps.

Although we haven't yet covered the range of financial returns that entrepreneurial real estate investors can earn, after you have read and mastered the techniques of financial analysis, you can revisit this issue. For now, just start thinking about goals. Then, as you read through later chapters, you can note the ideas that might work best for you. You will better remember and apply the ideas when you relate them to your own possibilities.

Set Up Your Investigation

Now that you "know thyself," it's time to set up your investigation of markets and properties. Before you take off to look at potential investments, define what you're looking for and what you're looking at:

- Explore the questions you want to answer.
- Identify the physical property.
- Identify the relevant property rights.
- Identify the area(s) from which you will draw customers (tenants, buyers) and identify the location and sources of potential competitors.
- What period of time defines your investment horizon (your holding period)?

Explore the Questions You Want to Answer

As a real estate entrepreneur, you'll face many questions that need answers. What's the market value of a specific property? Where's the market headed? What cities or neighborhoods offer good opportunities for growth? What cities or neighborhoods offer good cash flows? What market segments offer great potential? What features would bolster your MVP strategy? What lease terms could enhance the MVP strategy? How would the property's value go up if zoning were changed?

Throughout your career, you'll answer questions such as these as well as many similar ones. But you can't address all of them at the same time. Instead, focus. Each question requires its own data and methods. Market value questions, for example, differ from market forecasts. Cash flow questions differ from those that apply to appreciation potential.

You'll discover many more questions as you read through later chapters. Right now, recognize these three points:

1. Begin every investment decision with questions.
2. Never decide to buy, improve, or sell without looking at the property from multiple perspectives. (For example, that bargain price that looks so appealing may not compensate for weak cash flows or low potential for price growth—unless perhaps you plan to flip and take an immediate gain.)
3. The greater your ability to identify questions, the greater your profit potential. As we emphasize, questions alert you to opportunities that ordinary investors, property owners, and managers overlook. ("Could I get zoning changed?" "Could I split the lot?" "Could I go after the corporate rental market?" "Could I split the building into multiple units?" "Could I create a view?" Questions alert you to possibilities.)

Identify and Describe the Physical Property

It might surprise you to learn that when some investors buy a property, they do not know what they are getting. Why? Because they do not closely inspect the details of the property.

To prevent this mistake, here are the areas of inquiry you need to investigate:

- Number and mix of the rental units.
- Square footages of the total building and each rental unit.
- Site size, quality, boundaries, and amenities (fencing, landscaping, walkways, and so on).
- Type of construction, architectural style, and overall condition.
- Personal property.

As you look at a property from these different perspectives, identify defects and deficiencies. But also look for opportunities to create value. From one perspective, put on your Sherlock Holmes hat, take out your magnifying glass, and ferret out potential costly repairs, tenant turnover, or high energy bills. From the opportunity perspective, put on your rose-colored glasses. Imagine how the property could perform after you work your magic.

Number and Mix of Rooms and Rental Units

As with square footage (see the next section), sellers and their agents sometimes generously describe the number and mix of rental units within a building. I have seen so-called two-bedroom apartments that lacked closets, efficiencies that were nothing more than a sleeping room with a hot plate and dorm fridge, and damp, musty basement suites with no natural light.

Before you buy, inspect each unit in the property. Sometimes, agents (or sellers) will say, "The units are all *basically* alike; you don't want to look at all of them, do you?"

You should answer, "Yes, I think I do. You don't mind, do you?"

Square Footages

Agents and owners may quote two types of square-footage figures. One figure applies to the total size of the building. The other applies to the sizes of the individual units. The naive investor accepts these square-footage figures at face value. The smart investor questions the figures closely.

What areas are counted within the square footage figures? Apartment buildings, for example, devote space to hallways; basements; balconies; laundry facilities; heating, ventilating, and air-conditioning equipment; and the living units. Break down square-footage totals and allocate them across the building uses. Careful investigation requires this step for two reasons.

First, no consistent standard applies to square-footage measurements. Some owners or agents may count basements and balconies. Others may not. Precise allocations allow you to compare buildings. Second, note *rentable* square footage. Some buildings waste a lot of square footage because of inefficient design. A building of 13,500 square feet might actually include more *rentable* square feet than another property that measures 15,000 square feet. (The principle applies to single-family houses, office buildings, shopping centers, and industrial uses.)

Owners and agents sometimes like to promote their properties as a "great buy" because they compare favorably to the asking/sales prices of other properties on a price-per-square-foot basis. However, if the quality of that property's square footage appears inferior to its peer properties, then it deserves to sell at a discounted price per square foot. The lower asking price does not signal the great buy that the seller claims. Do not value all square footage equally.

Are the square footage figures accurate? Even though sellers and their agents nearly always hedge their estimates of square footage, beginning investors still too often rely on such figures only to learn too late that the figures erred. In instances where price per square foot counts heavily in your property comparisons and evaluations, pull out your tape measure. Figure the dimensions for yourself. Protect against the shock of fewer square feet than you bargained for—and thus a higher price per square foot than you thought you bargained for.

Site Size and Features

In many cities, the value of the lot on which a building sits can easily total 30 to 70 percent of the property's total value. Even small differences in site size or features can possibly add (or detract) tens of thousands of dollars compared with other, seemingly similar properties.

Consider two similar triplexes. Both properties brought in about the same amount of net rental income. Yet one triplex was listed at $289,000. The other was listed at $309,000. If you considered only the buildings, the $289,000 property looked like the better buy. But, in fact, the $309,000 property offered "hidden value" in the site. It turns out that this property's site size (and zoning) would permit its owner to build a fourth rental unit.

Additional site size might permit you to add on to a building, expand parking or storage space, create a view, or provide better privacy. To evaluate a site, take note of the quality of its landscaping, its ingress and egress (how easily cars can pull in and out of the property), and amenities such as swimming pool, tennis courts, workshop, or storage shed. When comparing size and features, itemize all those differences that can make a difference.

Personal Property

When you buy real estate, you pay for the land and the buildings, which are called *real property*. A seller's asking price might also include *personal property*, which refers to washers and dryers, refrigerators, stoves, furniture, curtains, blinds, window air-conditioning units, wall mirrors, and similar items not attached permanently to the land or building.

In addition, the list price for a property will include items that have been so adapted for use with the building that the law classifies these items as *fixtures*. Fixtures may include ceiling fans, lighting, chandeliers, garage door openers, garbage disposals, built-in cabinets and bookshelves, and built-in dishwashers. All other things equal, a property that includes a washer, dryer, ceiling fans, range, dishwasher, and refrigerator is worth more than one that omits such items. Before you value a property, itemize precisely the personal property and fixtures that the transaction includes. (Sometimes, after a sale, sellers remove fixtures even though legally they should remain with the property. For that reason and others, perform a final walk-through just before closing or taking possession.)

Avoid confusion and disappointment. Specifically negotiate "what stays with property, what goes with the sellers." Identify and list these items in your sales contract or attach with an addendum.

Understand Rights and Restrictions

"This is *my* property! I'll do with it whatever I want." In times that pre-date zoning restrictions, building codes, tenants' rights, mortgages, leases, and a multitude of other laws, ordinances, and contracts, your uncompromised claim to freedom may have carried weight. Not today.

Today, restrictions of one sort or another govern your rights to design, build, occupy, use, lease, mortgage, renovate, add on, or enjoy a property. Verify that your entrepreneurial plans for the properties you buy, manage, renovate, lease out, and sell comply with the legal rights that you actually possess (or can obtain).

On the other hand, zoning laws, contracts, ordinances, rules, covenants, and regulations do not merely restrict in a negative sense. Entrepreneurs rely on rules and restrictions to help fashion their target market strategy. Given the critical importance of this topic, we will discuss it in detail in Chapter 8. For now, realize that before you value a property and craft an MVP strategy, due diligence requires you to weigh and consider existing and potential restrictions.

What Geographic Area(s)?

Traditionally, most investors have often limited their search for properties to a geographic area that falls within a 30- to 60-minute radius of their home. These investors prefer to remain close to their properties so that they can easily deal with day-to-day issues (showing the property, making repairs, attending to tenants, and so on). Although their preference for proximity makes sense in some ways, it fails in others.

What if prices in your area sit beyond your reach? What if you can't find properties that yield positive cash flows or good potential for appreciation? What if your local economy looks shaky? In other words, what if your area seems to lack good investment alternatives that you are willing and able to buy? Now, maybe, you feel this way because you have not fully explored the possibilities in your locale. Maybe you've accepted conventional wisdom and negative self-talk without a detailed look at the facts.

Nevertheless, even if your locale offers more possibilities than you've discovered so far, open your mind to other geographic areas. During the next decade or two, real estate investors in some areas of the country will enjoy a doubling or tripling of their property values and rent levels. Property investors in other locales may do well to merely keep up with inflation. Or you might prefer to invest for cash flows more than appreciation. Here again, different locales offer different potential. As to my own investment objectives, I look for at least four good sources of return: (1) cash flows, (2) appreciation, (3) added value, and (4) amortization. In my view, many Texas and (noncoastal) Florida properties (commercial and residential) offer promise.

Of course, my point here is not to recommend a specific area. That's up to you to decide for yourself (with help from Chapter 5). However, I encourage you explore and compare a variety of locales. If you decide to invest locally, do it by design, not default.

Time Period

As part of your investment decision-making process, think about the length of time you plan to hold your properties. If you plan to fix and flip, your economic and market study need not forecast further out than 6 to 12 months. As a buy, improve, and hold investor, you would adopt a mid- to long-range perspective of, say, 5 to 20 years.

Different time perspectives lead to different investment choices. For example, many lower-priced neighborhoods and communities throughout the United States are primed for turnaround and attractive property appreciation. But these areas require a patient investor. To earn quick cash, find bargain-priced properties that you can fix up and immediately resell (or exchange). In any case, don't choose your locations or your properties until you think through the timing of your entrance and exit strategy.

Property prices and rent levels rarely follow a consistently upward-flowing trend line. Include timing as a critical part of your entrepreneurial strategy. Your MVP strategy for a two-year horizon could vary greatly from an MVP strategy that extends over 5 to 10 years. Plan your entry and exit.

Now, let's look more closely at the data you can use to forecast the demand and supply trends in an area.

6

WHERE'S THE AREA HEADED—AND WHEN?

LOOK BEYOND YOUR OWN BACKYARD

When Donald Trump began his career, he had his eye on Manhattan, not his native New York borough. He wanted to build in Manhattan because that's where he saw the greatest long-term opportunity to accomplish both his personal goals and financial objectives.

Today, the Trump Organization has been partners in U.S.-based projects in Miami, Tampa, Chicago, Phoenix, Las Vegas, Los Angeles, Palm Springs, and Atlantic City. Throughout the world, Trump now even has a project in Dubai, UAE (where I also have been doing some work over the past two years). As one of the fastest growing and wealthiest cities in the world, Dubai holds great long-term promise. Yet, until the Dubai ports political fury erupted, few Americans had heard of Dubai. "For a city where real estate is king" reads the promotional copy for Dubai's Palm Trump International Hotel and Tower, "now introducing the king of real estate."

What's the lesson? Avoid that tired cliché, "Never invest more than an hour's drive from your home." Throughout the United States, throughout the world, opportunities await those who will explore, investigate, and, yes, take a little risk. As Mr. Trump says, "Get out of your comfort zone, climb out to the edge."

Somewhere, real estate always offers exciting possibilities for profit. You can probably find acres of diamonds in your own backyard. But there's no need to only dig there. As Mr. Trump perpetually advises, "Think big."

Perhaps, like Mr. Trump, you, too, can develop a system that works superbly for a special niche of tenants or buyers. Perhaps you, too, can find partners to work with elsewhere. Challenge yourself to explore beyond your own backyard.

> **Location, location, location. That cliché is preached by know-nothings who fail to think. You're looking for the most profitable deal that might exist in any location. Plus, do what I do. Use your property to boost the value of the location.**

"THE AUTHOR DID IT—and so can you!" So opens the blurb page of the real estate classic *How I Turned $1,000 into a Million in My Spare Time* by William Nickerson. With these words of encouragement, I devoured the contents of this book. And at age 21, I began to immediately put Nickerson's advice into practice. I soon found (what I thought were) super bargains. According to Nickerson's formula, the price of rental property should equal 10 times that property's net operating income (NOI). Using this formula, I couldn't believe the fantastic deals that were coming my way. I routinely bought small apartment buildings for five to seven times NOI. In other words, I bought income properties that according to Nickerson's advice should have sold for $100,000. Yet I paid only $50,000 to $70,000.[1] Back then I thought, "These sellers are crazy. They don't know what they're doing."

ALAMO, CALIFORNIA (SAN FRANCISCO BAY AREA) VS. TERRE HAUTE, INDIANA

As it turned out, I was confused (not my sellers). I did not realize Nickerson's pricing formula did not apply to my hometown. Unlike the high-growth San Francisco Bay Area (where Nickerson lived), my hometown of Terre Haute suffered a frail local economy and a shrinking population. Whereas Nickerson's properties typically doubled in value over a period of 10 years, mine struggled to keep pace with inflation.

---

[1] These figures reflect proportionality, not the actual numbers.

Fortunately, my properties did yield huge amounts of positive cash flow, and because these beginning investment experiences predated the 1986 Tax Reform Act (TRA), my properties gave me huge tax write-offs for depreciation. Using this tax shelter, I enjoyed tax-free income from both my property rent collections and most of my professional earnings.

This comparison of locales shows that you need to weigh the pros and cons of an area's growth and appreciation potential against the area's property prices and cash flows.

Two Common Mistakes

Some investors (both beginning and seasoned) search for properties to buy in an area (region, city, neighborhood) without much thought about how that area might eventually compare to other areas 3, 5, 10, or maybe 15 years into the future. Typically, these investors focus on buying properties that look like a good deal here and now. I call this practice the Mr. Magoo mistake. It's too nearsighted. (I made the Mr. Magoo mistake.)

In contrast to Mr. Magoo, others (such as today's San Francisco investors) buy properties located in high-growth areas—especially areas where properties have shown strong past rates of economic growth and price appreciation. These investors seem to care little about today's negative cash flows because they assume that future rates of appreciation will mirror the past. I call this practice the stargazer mistake. It's too hopefully farsighted.

Relatively Speaking, Not Absolute

In most cases (but by no means all), both Mr. Magoo and stargazer types of property investors have made money. When I say "mistake," I speak relatively, not absolutely. (I suspect that most stock and bond investors would have loved my returns of 30 percent or more.) I am saying that these "mistaken" property investors (myself included) often took on more risk and received less reward than we could have earned had we adopted a more reasoned choice of areas and properties.

Today, I favor an approach called *right place, right time, right price* investing.

VALUE INVESTING: RIGHT PLACE, RIGHT TIME, RIGHT PRICE

If you're familiar with the various styles of investing that stock market enthusiasts adopt, you might recognize right place, right time, right price investing as similar to value investing (see my book *Value Investing in Real Estate*).

A value investor in stocks never buys into a company simply because it's a great company. Nor will he buy just any company even if its stock price is low relative to its earnings and dividends (annual cash flow). For the value investor to buy, he needs the right company, at the right time, at the right price.

Value Investing in Real Estate

Similarly, as a value investor in real estate, you search for areas (right places) that are positioned for growth, turnaround, gentrification, or revitalization. You next ask, "Is this the right time?" Harlem was positioned for turnaround in the early 1980s. But its renaissance did not begin to take off for another 10 to 12 years. Throughout the 1980s, Harlem suffered from drugs, crime, and further deterioration—even though it was located just minutes from high-income job, shopping, and apartment districts.

In 1990, San Diego was the right place to invest, but like Harlem of the 1980s, the timing for investment wasn't right. As one of the most desirable places to live in the world, no one could deny the solid long-term prospects for "America's number one city."

The short term, though, raised more troubling issues. As a major center for defense-related jobs, San Diego was about to suffer a steep increase in unemployment because the fall of the Soviet threat foreshadowed a rollback of military spending in the U.S. budget. The San Diego property market would drop before it would regain its predictably bright long-term future.

To profit most in real estate, look for areas (countries, regions, cities, neighborhoods) that are both positioned and *poised* for growth, turnaround, gentrification, or revitalization. Look for able and *ready*. The right time matters.

What about Price?

In my right place, right time, right price trilogy, you can think about right price in four ways:

1. *Market Value:* Never pay a price that exceeds market value unless you know precisely why you can justify your price premiums.
2. *Premium Value:* On occasion, you can afford to sensibly (if you have to) pay a premium above market value to acquire a property you want. Several such reasons might include favorable terms or costs of financing, conversion possibilities, special use potential, and value-added potential.
3. *Price Trends:* An area can stand positioned and poised for growth, but current market prices could tumble over the short run. A steep upward spike in interest rates, a surfeit of new construction, excess numbers of conversions, or a legislative or regulatory change, such as the 1986 TRA, might bring about a temporary stall or fall in property prices.
4. *Price to Earnings:* Since the early 2000s, many properties (especially in much-sought-after locations) failed to yield positive cash flows when financed with a 30-year fixed-rate loan with

a 20 percent down payment. For this reason, many value investors typically avoid such areas as "wrong price"—no matter how otherwise desirable the area appears.

Look for properties in marginal areas that are located near more appealing areas. These properties stand a good chance of appreciating.

SUMMING UP: RIGHT PLACE, RIGHT TIME, RIGHT PRICE

Mr. Magoo focuses on the specific property deal. For this type of investor, a "good buy" is nearly any property that's priced well below its current market value. As a result of his nearsightedness, Mr. Magoo frequently misses properties in areas positioned and posed for growth. In addition, because Mr. Magoo pays slight attention to economic and market outlooks, he can fail to notice market data that signal imminent price declines.

I'll ask the people who live nearby about an area—schools, crime, shopping, whatever. I ask cabdrivers, postmen, FedEx guys. I ask, ask, ask, until I hone my analytics as well as my instincts. Then, I decide.

Stargazers presume to see the prospects for property prices for the areas where they invest. But (like Magoos), they can drown in a whirlpool of downward trends. Or waiting for future rescue, stargazers get eaten by alligators. Their negative cash flows consume most (or all) of the profits they had counted on from property appreciation.

Although no one can perfectly predict the future, value (entrepreneurial) investors typically make the best forecasts and most profitable decisions. Rather than assume the short- or long-term future of an area, rather than choose their areas or properties by default (close to home, strong past rate of appreciation, below-market price), value investors carefully answer these three questions:

1. Where's the right place (country, region, city, neighbor-hood) to invest?
2. When's the right time to invest?
3. What's the right price to pay?

Demand

Unlike the media molls who offer up stale back-of-the-envelope conventional wisdom, you can reasonably figure the prospects for an area. Before making an investment decision, review these types of big-picture (macro) indicators of demand (the D of DUST):

I. Demand.
   a. Population growth.
   b. Employment and incomes.
   c. Costs of doing business.
   d. Quality of life.
   e. Wealth.
   f. Community attitudes.
   g. Entrepreneurial spirit.

By itself, strong growing demand within an area does not guarantee a profit. Also review indicators of supply (the S in DUST), such as the following:

II. Supply: Review potential competitors.
   a. New construction.
   b. Existing homes for sale.
   c. Existing homes for rent.
   d. Condos for sale.

    e. Condos for rent.
    f. Apartment vacancy rates.
    g. Apartment rent levels.
    h. Available buildable land.
    i. Zoning and land use restrictions.
    j. Delinquencies and mortgage foreclosures.

You will discover how to review the indicators of supply (competitors) in a later chapter. Now, on with a macro look at demand.

As a beginning investor, you may want to skip over technical talk about economic base, market signals, demand, and supply. "Just tell me what I need to know to make a lot of money." But until you check the facts about your local area (or the local area where you plan to invest), you're aiming without a sight. You may hit your target, but, then again, you may not. Even when you score a sequence of hits, don't get too cocky about your successes (as we all are prone to do). While you're enjoying your rewards, someone just might move the target.

Donald Trump admits to this mistake in the late 1980s. He lost his focus, but not just by jumping from deal to deal; he let the good times roll. Then trouble hit. As he tells the story, he had "fun, fun, fun, until the banks took the Gulfstream away." Stay focused. Continually monitor demand and competition (supply). As times change, adjust your strategy and your debt loads.

WILL THE POPULATION GROW?

Population growth (or decline) results from three sources: (1) births, (2) mortality, and (3) people moving into or out of an area. Get a clear picture of an area. Are more people moving in, or are they moving away? How is the age distribution of the population changing? Most people think of Florida as Heaven's waiting room. But the number of children in the state is growing fast. If the number of seniors flooding into the state should stop (which will not happen), playgrounds full of today's children will provide tomorrow's demand for apartments, houses, retail sites, and office buildings.

Pockets of Existing and Potential Growth

Population growth seldom spreads itself evenly across states, cities, or neighborhoods. Geographic areas develop pockets or corridors of growth. Determine where the heaviest growth has occurred. Is this area reaching its limit? Are the roads and freeways choking with traffic? Have rents and housing prices shot upward? Where will the next burst of population increase occur? Look for emerging areas.

Find out the Actual Numbers

Sometimes the media report that the population growth *rate* of an area is slowing. Most people interpret this news to mean that growth *itself* is slowing. Often that's not the case. Rather, as the population of an area gets larger, the percentage increase can fall even though the number of people moving in continues to increase.

Say that during the past decade the population of a county jumped from 300,000 to 400,000—an overall growth of 33 percent. During the coming decade, this overall growth rate is expected to fall to 25 percent. Nevertheless, even with this lower growth rate, the county population will increase by 100,000, exactly the same *number* of people as in the previous decade. It is the *number* of people who create demand, not the percentage growth rate per se. Watch the numbers.

Beware of False Negatives

If you look at the population growth figures within the city limits of Highland Park, Texas; San Francisco; Washington, D.C.; or New York City; you would note little upward change in numbers during the past 30 years. Yet housing prices and rent levels in each of these cities have climbed to rank among the highest in the United States. Why? Because these cities draw their demand through their larger metro areas, the country, and the world. To judge the total demand for housing in a specific community or neighborhood, study the projected population growth figures for entire contiguous areas. Evaluate big-picture (macro) influences on smaller areas.

ARE THE NUMBER OF BASIC JOBS INCREASING OR DECREASING?

To grow and prosper, most (but not all) areas need a core of *basic* employment. (Property prices in Aspen, Colorado, have increased 10 times over without significant gains in high-income employment. Wealthy out-of-area buyers account for most of the demand.) Identify an area's major employers, the predominant types of businesses, and their potential for growth. On the downside, investigate whether any cutbacks, layoffs, plant closings, or business relocations appear on the horizon.

Specifically, basic employers are those types of activities that bring money into an area. When these businesses decline, so do all the nonbasic businesses that feed off the revenues generated by these core firms (or government agencies and institutions). Basic employment typically includes the following:

1. *Manufacturers:* To see the critical role that manufacturers play, watch the Michael Moore movie *Roger and Me*. This documentary catalogs the economic downfall of Flint, Michigan, after General Motors closed the local Buick plant.

2. *Professional Service Firms:* Most low- and mid-level architects, lawyers, accountants, consultants, and advertising agencies count only as town fillers, not town builders. Classified similarly are real estate agents, stockbrokers, and insurance agencies. However, some professional (or financial) service firms cater to a regional, statewide, national, or even global clientele. The billings of these firms may bring millions (or even billions) of dollars into a local economy. Think of Chicago's

Skidmore Owens, the internationally respected architectural firm that's designing the world's tallest building under construction in Dubai.

3. *Medical Services:* Health care has become the second largest business (behind real estate) in the United States and will become much larger as the baby boomers hit their 60s. Many local areas now provide hospitals, clinics, and testing labs that bring in patients from hundreds (or even thousands) of miles away. Think Mayo Clinic.

4. *Travel and Tourism:* It seems like nearly every urban and rural area in the country now wants to capture part of the $300 billion a year that Americans spend on travel, tourism, conventions, and other leisure-related activities. Think Chicago's McCormick Place or San Francisco's Moscone Center.

5. *Colleges and Universities:* Many towns and cities are home to colleges or universities that bring millions (or billions) into the local area. (Boston, for example, is home to 62 colleges.) College-related spending in the small town of Bloomington, Indiana, tops $2 billion a year.

6. *Retailing and Distribution:* The Omni shopping center in Miami attracts shoppers who live in Mexico, Brazil, and Argentina. Honey Creek Mall in Terre Haute, Indiana, draws shoppers from the surrounding rural areas and small towns up to 60 miles away. The corner grocery does not support an area's economic base. But large shopping malls, catalog centers, and warehousing operations (e.g., Amazon.com, L.L. Bean) can employ hundreds (or even thousands) based on revenues received from throughout the region, the country, or the world. The Sawgrass Mall near Miami, Florida, pulls in millions of shoppers a year.

7. *Centers of Government:* Capital cities generate revenues from throughout their respective jurisdictions. Washington, D.C., and Ottawa draw in tax dollars from throughout the United States and Canada, respectively. Other cities bring in revenues from state and federal agencies, military bases, defense

contractors, and VA hospitals that are located in the area. Think NASA and Titusville, Florida.

Few small investors pay much attention to their area's basic employment—unless their economy has already turned into recession. When the southern California economy boomed in the late 1980s, stargazer investors and home buyers imagined that property appreciation rates of 10 to 20 percent a year would last forever. When the Berlin Wall fell in 1989, few potential buyers anticipated any effects on San Diego home prices and apartment rents.

What Was the Connection?

As I mentioned, U.S. spending for defense supported thousands of basic jobs in southern California. After the Berlin Wall fell, Congress quite predictably slashed defense spending. Defense contractors, in turn, slashed tens of thousands of jobs. Congress also cut back the number of personnel stationed at the San Diego Naval Base.

When employment fell, demand for homes and apartments fell. Nearly everyone connected with home building and home selling began to feel the effects. Home builders shut down their construction sites. Most real estate agents, mortgage loan reps, home inspectors, property lawyers, title insurers, and apartment managers experienced cuts in income. These depressing effects further rippled through the local economy.

Forecast Recovery

At that time, I was living in Berkeley, California, and frequently flew down to La Jolla (near San Diego) for weekend excursions. I kept my eye on market signals firsthand. By the mid-1990s, everything was in place. The market had hit bottom. Both population and job growth were turning from negative to positive. Mortgage lenders were making it easier to borrow.

That's when I wrote, "By the year 2001, many renters through-out Southern California will sorely regret the housing bargains they missed during the mid-1990s (*Stop Renting Now*, p. 161). Yet, as of 1996, a so-called real estate expert for *The San Francisco Examiner* wrote, "A home is where the bad investment is" (November 17, 1996). And another California expert wrote, "The quick buck prof-its [in real estate] are long gone. . . . Buying a property in excellent condition and hoping somehow to earn a profit is a no-win situa-tion" (*San Diego Union-Tribune*, September 8, 1996).

Why could I see what others missed? Because I know how to read and weigh market signals. And that's a skill that you can learn. Magoos and stargazers alike tend to stretch the present or recent past into the future. Likewise, several years back, stock market enthusiasts all fore-casted stock market gains of 10 to 15 percent annually. (Do you recall the then best-selling books *Dow 36,000* and *Stocks for the Long Run*?) Following the past alone, stock speculators failed to comprehend the multiple facts that signaled a crash in the tech stocks and dot-coms.

Neither I nor anyone else can *precisely* forecast when and by how much home prices (or rents) will increase or decrease. But you do not need *precision*. You need to monitor fundamentals of demand and supply. Then adjust your strategy.

In November 1996, Robert Shiller (author of *Irrational Exuberance*) began his long-running critique of the stock market frenzy. Even in 1996, stock prices were out of whack with corporate earnings and dividends. Yet the major stock market indexes continued to shoot up until early 2000. Even so, by 2003, those investors who had heeded Schiller's warnings in 1997 or 1998 (and moved their money into bonds or real estate) were far ahead of those stock investors who refused to change their investment strategy.

COST OF RUNNING A BUSINESS

Why did the old-time New England textile manufacturers move their factories to the South? Why did many Silicon Valley technology firms move all or part of their operations to Austin, Texas? Why did my publisher, John Wiley & Sons, Inc., recently give up its long-time world headquarters at 605 Third Avenue, New York City, in favor of a new office complex just across the Hudson River in Hoboken, New Jersey? Why do savvy real estate entrepreneurs forecast huge growth in warehousing and distribution employment along the I-4 corridor that links Daytona Beach, Orlando, and Tampa–St. Petersburg, Florida? Costs. Lower costs of running a business.

Businesses and Employment Migrate to Lower-Cost Cities, States, and Countries

In the highly competitive national and global marketplace, major firms persistently scout for business locations that will reduce their costs of labor, transportation, real estate, energy, and taxes. In addition, they look to see what kinds of incentives government(s) might provide, such as worker training, low-interest financing, and tax abatements.

This search at times may simply encourage a move from the central business core to the suburbs or perhaps across state lines to a more tax-friendly environment. On other occasions, the move may take the firm's jobs to a different state or country. Overall, you need to size up the relative cost competitiveness of the area(s) where you plan to invest. Do you think that its cost structure (on balance) will encourage employers to move in—or push them to move out?

Cost of Living for Employees

Basic employers also factor in an area's costs of living for their employees. The quip in Silicon Valley for the past several years has been, "What do you call an engineer who earns $150,000 a year?" Answer: A renter. Given the outrageously high living costs (especially housing prices but also California state income taxes, traffic congestion, and auto and homeowners insurance), many Silicon Valley firms will need to find alternative locations that provide a more affordable lifestyle for employees.

In the past, Seattle and Austin attracted tech firms that wanted to offer their employees an area with a lower cost of living. While still cheaper than Silicon Valley, these cities no longer offer the clear-cut advantages they displayed at the start of the 1990s. So the question now becomes: Where are the next hot spots for tech (or other types of employment) that will grow strongly in the future? Salt Lake City? Pittsburgh? Chapel Hill? Atlanta? Champaign–Urbana? Where does your knowledge or research lead you to look?

QUALITY OF LIFE

Today, people choose places to live and work to enjoy the quality of life. Executives evaluate new locations on the basis of climate, recreational activities, school systems, cultural facilities, municipal services, crime rates, housing costs, and traffic congestion.

Before you buy, ask, "Will this area improve with time? Will the area become more desirable, or less?"

Many communities that seek growth try to build their quality-of-life images. A passage from an Edmonton, Alberta, economic brochure reads as follows:

> The distinct seasons enjoyed by Edmontonians are indicative of the recreational activities available. Summers are warm, with daytime temperatures averaging 22°C (72°F) and evening temperatures cooling to a pleasant 15°C (60°F). Summer is complemented by a mild spring and autumn, as well as plenty of sunshine, making much of the year enjoyable for hiking, cycling, trail riding, golf, tennis and camping. Trails for bicycles and

hiking in Capital City Park are linked by four pedestrian foot-bridges across the North Saskatchewan River. Along this river valley are adjacent golf courses, boat launches, picnic sites and a beautiful network of trails. . . .

To complement the pleasant summers and invigorating winters, Edmonton offers virtually pollution-free and pollen-free air. Edmonton is a city to be enjoyed by all, for all seasons.

Have the city boosters aroused your desire to seek a job or start a business in Edmonton? During the coming years, cities that achieve economic growth will also be those that can sell their advantages as a good place to raise a family and enjoy life. How do the areas rate that attract your interest? What serious efforts (if any) are being made to improve them?

Quality of Life Also Attracts Wealth

Who are the people who have bought property in Aspen, Colorado; Jackson Hole, Wyoming; Longboat Key, Florida; Banner Elk, North Carolina; Ashland, Oregon; or Sedona, Arizona? They're not the people who currently hold jobs in those areas. They're people with high incomes or wealth who choose where they want to live (or own a second home). Increasingly, too, free agents (writers, artists, consultants, inventors, programmers, entrepreneurs) enjoy the money and occupational freedom to set up their lifestyle wherever it suits them.

Cities, towns, and even rural communities that appeal to the footloose and financially mobile will continue to experience high demand for their residential properties. This trend is here to stay. As boomers head into retirement and the Internet (and employer intranet) revolution permits increasing numbers of people to work from home—no matter where that home is located—people will abandon high-cost, low-quality-of-life areas in favor of those areas where they want to live. What areas do you know that will attract these growing market segments?

Community Attitudes and Actions

Another factor that boosts demand and explains why some areas grow faster than others is community attitudes. Do the city leaders promote economic growth?

Not All Areas Seek Growth

In some states and cities, the answer to this question is "no." Sometimes local business or government leaders discourage new firms from locating in an area as a way to protect vested interests. Sometimes local politicians develop a power base that they do not want outsiders to challenge. The local citizenry may want to preserve a way of life.[2] Through elected and appointed officials, they make it difficult for new firms to obtain permits, licenses, and zoning approval.[3] In the past—and especially in towns dominated by one or several major employers—powerful owners of existing firms have successfully kept new industry out of an area. Their real reason has been to avoid additional bidders for available workers and thereby maintain low wage rates.

Growth Sought

In cities that want economic growth, firms, private organizations, and various government officials actively recruit investment and new employers. For example, the Jacksonville Chamber of Commerce hired a national consulting firm to prepare a comprehensive economic

---

[2] During the late 1970s, Oregon opposed economic growth quite loudly, even to the extent of advertising Oregon as a state where newcomers were not welcome. By 1984, tough political leaders and citizens had changed their tune. Badly hurt by the recession of 1981-1982 and still slow to recover, Oregon went out recruit new industry.

[3] Recently, the city fathers in Terre Haute turned away 400 high-paying jobs because local power brokers opposed the company (a major chaemical manufacturer).

analysis of that city. The study sought to identify the types of employers whose needs would best match Jacksonville's strengths. In addition, the consultant recommended ways that Jacksonville community leaders could improve the marketing of the city to targeted employers. Similarly, two rapidly growing areas in North America have been Calgary and Edmonton, Alberta, Canada. Although their economies benefited from the well-endowed resource base of Alberta (especially oil and farmland), a contributing factor has also been the pro-business, pro-growth attitude of the provincial and city governments. In Canada, a country where left-leaning political attitudes tend to dominate, Alberta has gained a reputation for free enterprise.

Entrepreneurial Spirit

Professor Jeanne Biggar traced the shifts in population that the United States has experienced since 1970. She noted that 15 Sunbelt states had accounted for nearly two-thirds of America's population growth. Biggar pointed out, however, that the real meaning of these shifts was not so much the number of people who were moving to the South and West; it was the *quality* of those who migrated that spelled decline for the older cities. "The industrial North," Professor Biggar found, "is losing the able young who might be most likely to provide the creative ideas and enthusiastic leadership needed to tackle the problems associated with deteriorating cities"—in other words, those who approach life with what I call an *entrepreneurial attitude*.

Many older cities are *not* declining because they are losing their economic base; rather, they are losing their economic base because they are losing the individuals who could breathe life into their economies. No city, no state, and no country can create or sustain prosperity unless it nourishes entrepreneurs who remain alert to changing markets, who can discover opportunities, and who can combine resources in new and better ways to create value for others.

Regardless of an area's advantages, the drive of its people will determine its prosperity. Do the people who live (or are moving into the area) display the entrepreneurial spirit? Look for areas that attract entrepreneurial talent.

Summing Up

When I began to buy properties in my hometown, I knew nothing about the city's economic base. Quite likely, I couldn't have told you what the term *economic base* meant. But since then, I have witnessed booms, busts, and recoveries in Dallas, Texas; San Diego, California; and Vancouver, British Columbia. I know that a strong local economy can help turn real estate investors into multimillionaires and that a slide (even when temporary) can turn unprepared investors upside down and shake their pockets empty.

Even if you're a short-term fix and flipper, regularly monitor an area's basic sources of jobs, income, wealth, and quality of life. If the economic signals start flashing yellow, pay attention. Don't think you can blindly speed through without danger.

Use your knowledge of economic base to help you select geographic areas and communities that show long-run promise. Discover those cities, suburbs, or even neighborhoods that will experience high rates of growing demand over the next 5, 10, or 15 years. Had I understood the basics of what I have laid out for you in this chapter at the start of my career, I would have chosen to invest somewhere other than Terre Haute. Or perhaps I would have targeted a more promising part of the Terre Haute urban area than those neighborhoods where I actually did buy. At the least, I would have recognized that my properties were unlikely to achieve the same rates of appreciation as those properties in California. Properties across the United States—or even throughout the same metro area—seldom increase in value at a uniform pace. Those properties appreciate fastest where future demand will push against a constrained supply of competitors.

Put this knowledge to work. In the words of Donald Trump, "Before you invest, you've got to know your territory."

7

CREATE MARKET SEGMENTS

**My father offered a top product to working people
who had lived their whole lives in cramped, crowded
rental apartments: modestly priced, suburban-style
brick houses. His buyers bought them faster than
he could build them. He knew his customers just as
well as I know mine.**

P OPULATION GROWTH, JOBS, incomes, wealth, quality of life—
these and other macro demand factors (Chapter 6) begin your
study of an area. However, in today's world of real estate, diversity
rules. To maximize your entrepreneurial profits, explore and create
market segments. What features and services can you provide to
achieve a competitive advantage for tenants or buyers who express
similar—yet hard-to-find—needs, wants, desires, and preferences?

DIVERSITY RULES

True diversity includes a panorama of demographics and psychographics (feelings, lifestyles, and attitudes). The features of a property I like may not appeal to you. The features you like may not
appeal to someone else. When you notice how people differ in their
likes and dislikes and what they're willing to pay for, you can zero in
on a select bull's-eye of tenants or buyers.

**Even if your customers don't make as much money
as mine do, still make your property seem special
to them. That's what my father and I did with
Swifton Village.**

DEMOGRAPHIC DIFFERENCES

Think about the following list of demographic characteristics. Think
how you might use one or more of these to segment a market. With

these attributes in mind, craft a strategy to meet a motivating need, want, or problem of these people. What properties have you noticed that cater to certain types of buyers or tenants? What idea can you generate?

- Young professional.
- College student.
- Female, male.
- Occupation/employer.
- Retiree.
- Nonsmokers.
- Disability.
- Neighborhood.
- Household size (number of persons).
- Household composition (characteristics of household members).
- Income/credit score.
- Wealth/cash savings.
- Stage of life.
- Religion/ethnicity.
- Credit score.
- Home owner/renter.
- Marital status.

Here are several examples from my experience. (Note: Before you develop your market segmentation strategy, make sure you do not violate fair housing laws.)

Share-a-Home (Age and Health)

Among my properties, I formerly owned a 3,200-square-foot, five-bedroom, four-bath, single-family house that I rented out for $850 a month to a married couple with children. In talking with another property owner in the neighborhood (always searching for ideas),

I discovered a more profitable use for that house, that is, a better MVP (most valued property) strategy.

It turned out that this investor owned four properties and rented rooms in each of these large houses to individual seniors. Typically, these people were age 70 or older. They were healthy enough to care for their own basic everyday living but not up to maintaining their own private residence. The investor essentially operated these properties as high-class boardinghouses. He called these houses share-a-homes. Previously, I had not heard of this type of tenant segmentation strategy.

In following up on this idea, I learned that blind luck favored me. Not only was my property located within a share-a-home zoning district, but also, with no changes whatsoever, the property met the strict regulatory housing codes that applied for this use (e.g., size of bedrooms, number of bathrooms, number and location of exits, window locks, kitchen facilities). Although I had no interest in personally managing a share-a-home, I did lease the house to the operator down the street. My new rent: $1,350 per month. He then leased out each bedroom at around $600 a month for a total rent collection of $2,400.

Share-a-Home Update: Tropical Village, Inc.

Along these same lines, a development project called Tropical Village has updated and upgraded the share-a-home market segmentation strategy. Here's an excerpt from one of its promotional letters:

> There is no other product in the rental market within our rent range that offers the amenities [fitness center, heated swimming pool, beauty salon, card and Super Bowl room, putting green, shuffleboard, maid service] that we are offering. Our target market for rental is the senior that cannot quite handle the daily upkeep of a home or apartment, yet they are healthy and are not ready for the assisted living type of care.... Seniors can keep their independence longer.

Tropical Village provides a value proposition that many seniors prefer. Given the success of their previous share-a-home developments, they have clearly achieved a competitive advantage over more generic rental properties.

OTHER MARKET SEGMENT POSSIBILITIES

You can slice and dice demographics in thousands of different combinations. Because you're renting out (or selling) one property at a time, you can pinpoint the needs of a quite narrow type of person, family, or household. Obviously, Donald Trump's strategies appeal to those very wealthy who value status. One renovator I knew specifically tailored his rental properties to better accommodate roommate living, families with young children, or families with teenage children. Wheelchair-friendly units also seem to be in short supply relative to demand. Some property owners target the financially responsible yet cash- or credit-impaired renter. One of my previous properties was located two blocks from a hospital. I fixed up the property and drafted a rental agreement that, when brought together, made these units especially appealing to single nurses.

Psychographic Differences

Most large developers, home builders, and apartment complexes combine demographics with psychographics to create their target markets. In this sense, I'm using the term *psychographics* to refer to all types of mental predispositions, such as likes, dislikes, tastes, preferences, attitudes, values, and lifestyle. Again quoting from a Tropical Village promotional letter,

> Our goal is to offer safe and affordable housing to the healthy, active senior. Many seniors have a major problem with loneliness and lack of interaction with other people. . . . [Therefore]

seniors like this shared living concept. . . . and generally form little family-type groups. . . . We are able to sponsor a program of activities for our residents.

From this passage, you can see how Tropical Village blends demographic characteristics, such as age and health, with psychographic characteristics, such as active lifestyle, social interaction, and safety. Notice how the firm is trying to understand the needs and wants of its target audience and craft its apartment units, amenities, and services to meet those needs.

I know my customers. I'm not going for the old wealth that dates back to the Rockefellers and duPonts. My target is the rich Italian with the beautiful wife and the red Ferrari. That's the audience that Trump Tower was designed for.

Myrtle Beach Condominiums

Some years back, I was called in as a marketing research consultant by a developer in Myrtle Beach, South Carolina, who was trying to get financing to build a condominium project. Unfortunately for this developer, mortgage lenders thought he was nuts. At that time, the national economy was mired in a deep recession. Gasoline prices were shooting up, and, of no small concern, the local Myrtle Beach housing market was littered with unsold see-through, midrise, beachfront condo projects.[1]

But this developer wasn't crazy. He had studied his market segment. He knew that as one of the premier golfing centers in the United States, Myrtle Beach attracted hundreds of thousands of visitors each year who cared nothing about the Atlantic Ocean and Grand Strand beaches. These visitors come to play golf all day

---

[1] A "see-through" building is a partially built, abandoned project. Since only the skeleton (frame) of the building has been put up, you can see right through it.

and dine on seafood, drink, and share camaraderie with friends all evening. These golfing buddies didn't need or want an expensive beachfront condo (or hotel). They wanted comfortable, private, and spacious accommodations at an affordable price.

The developer's value proposition: a 1,350-square-foot, town-house style, two-bedroom, two-bath condo, located 14 blocks west of the beach yet within 15 minutes of most popular golf courses. Because of this "off-the-beaten-path" site, the developer could price the units for 60 percent less than the condos that created the beachfront bust. Yet that wasn't the end of the story.

The developer knew that many golfing buddies circulate within a group of 6 to 10 (or more) friends. To make the condo units more economical, he promoted joint ownership among perhaps 4, 6, or even 10 partners. With this type of purchase plan, he significantly increased the number of potential buyers for his units. The golfing buddies were able to obtain housing that surpassed the quality of anything comparable in the market. But when figured on a per-person, nightly-use basis, it cost less than a Holiday Inn.

Within 18 months, the developer had sold out the first two phases of the project and was already into planning the third. In this case, savvy target marketing and product development created huge profits for this astute entrepreneur—when most other builders were going broke. Even "oversupply" doesn't foreclose opportunity.

AVOID STANDARD LABELS, PICTURE YOUR ACTUAL RENTERS

You may have heard people refer to housing segments such as empty-nesters, yuppies, first-time home buyers, move-up buyers, the age 55+ market, and, more recently, the Hispanic market, the Asian market, and even the Islamic market. SRI (formerly known as the Stanford Research Institute, a Menlo Park firm with which I've done some consulting work) developed a market segment classification system known as VALS (an acronym for values and lifestyles) that was *unthinkingly* relied on by some apartment complexes and home builders. SRI's staff placed much of the U.S. population into the following market segments:

- Survivors.
- Sustainers.
- Achievers.
- Belongers.
- Emulators.
- Societally conscious.

Although any or all of these labels might stimulate your thinking, never let mere labels to shape your market segmentation strategy. One book for real estate investors tells its readers to sell their renovated properties to first-time home buyers. But that label (as do all generic segmentation labels) lacks clarity and precision. I learned that fact during the 1990s, when I was offering my Stop Renting Now! seminars throughout the country. My seminar attendees fit no specific demographic. They included a wide range of ages, income, wealth, and family size:

- Age (25 to 55).
- Income ($20,000 to $120,000).
- Cash down available (0 to $100,000).
- Credit record, from excellent to lousy.
- Family status (single, divorced, separated, married, married with children, unmarried partners).
- Race (all races).
- Lifestyles (all the values, attitudes, and life situations that anyone could imagine).

However, all these people did hold one motivating preference in common. They wanted to stop renting and start owning. When you create a target market for your properties, think precisely. Picture clearly in relevant detail the characteristics (demographics, psychographics, lifestyles, preferences, turn-ons, and turnoffs) of the people for whom you would like to create their MVP. Then design the features of your property and leasing program to motivate your customers to act (rent or buy).

COLLEGE STUDENTS

I've heard owners of rental houses and apartments declare that they avoid renting to "college students." But like first-time home buyers, college students come in all types. I once renovated a 16-unit apartment building specifically for a target market of college students. That building proved profitable, and the students appreciated the way management ran the property to serve their preferences.

But we didn't rent to just any college students. We targeted top students who were nonsmokers, had above-average financial resources, and were mature in demeanor, quiet, and clean. In return, we offered the most pleasant place to live at a fair rent level. We achieved extraordinary profits through lower costs for repairs, marketing, and management as well as virtually zero vacancies and bad debts. We achieved MVP status.

HIT THE BULL'S-EYE

You might first think about target marketing with broad-brush labels such as sustainers, achievers, college students, first-time buyers, active seniors, empty-nesters, young marrieds, roommates, singles, moderate income, or even that once ubiquitous segment known as yuppies (who now have become aging boomers).

Any broad-brush label might point you toward market segments that share some similar characteristics. But the hearts and minds within each of these generalized categories also show differences that make a difference. To hit that most profitable bull's-eye within your market segment, search for the unique and intense needs that best motivate select types of people. What features and benefits would really motivate your prospects?

FIND UNIQUE AND INTENSE NEEDS

To create your MVP, find those intense (motivating) needs and wants that most other competing property owners are missing. Identify your tenants' (buyers') hot buttons. I found that the nurses I rented to were worried about safety and security. So I increased the amount of outdoor lighting at the property, installed double-deadbolt door locks, and placed heavy-gauge wire mesh screens on the building's first-story windows.

These nurses also wanted more closet space than the other older rental units in the neighborhood typically provided. Fortunately, the bedrooms in my property measured at least 14 by 16 feet. That feature allowed me to slice off two feet of floor space and add a wall-length closet in each bedroom. As a special touch, I installed full-length mirrors on the new closet doors. This not only played to vanity but also gave the bedrooms a spacious appearance.

INDIVIDUAL LEASES

In taking a cue from Doreen Brierbrier (*Managing Your Rental Property for More Income*), I rented to the nurses individually rather than as a preformed group. I also permitted any nurse to get out of her lease at any time if she would find a substitute tenant who proved acceptable to me and the existing residents of the house. These (primarily younger) women appreciated that flexibility— although few exercised this option. In fact, the low tenant turnover at that property actually surprised me.

THROW AWAY STANDARD OPERATING PROCEDURES

Most owners of small rental properties operate their buildings according to some combination of standard operating procedure, the detailed directions offered by authors of their favorite real estate books, or the owner's personal insights and idiosyncratic prejudices, unguided by a customer (tenant) profile. I urge you to practice a more profitable approach. Get to know your intended customer. My experiences and the experiences of other entrepreneurs prove that the more closely you identify and attend to the motivating needs of potential tenants, the more they will reward you with a higher and more dependable stream of rental income (MVP applies to you, too).

Contrary to the principles of target marketing, owners who merely offer a generic rental property to a generic tenant earn (at best) generic returns. When you follow their example, you condemn yourself to so-called market rent levels—for that's what "market" refers to: the average rent for a standard, look-alike product in an open and competitive marketplace. No MVP entrepreneur competes with a plain-Jane generic product.

How Do You Identify the Wow (MVP) Features for Your Tenants?

Since you can't read minds, you need some techniques to discover those elements of your value proposition that will motivate your customers to act now. Here are several methods that have worked for me and other entrepreneurial property investors:

- Talk informally with people; discover their problems.
- Pay attention, eavesdrop, read, watch.
- Talk with insiders and experts.
- Conduct (informal) focus groups.

Informal Conversations

I'm an inquisitor. No matter where I am, I like to strike up conversations with people to learn their thoughts, problems, likes, and dislikes. In fact, I discovered the housing opportunity for nurses while visiting one of my parents in the hospital. In casual conversation, I asked a nurse where she lived. That opened the door to one of those "Don't get me started on that" comments.

That backhanded invitation intensified my inquiry and led to further conversation with the nurse. She then went on to describe how much difficulty she and her workmates encountered when looking for a decent and affordable place to live near the hospital—which is where they preferred to live given their odd-hour work schedules. People know what they want, so ask them.

Similarly, because I've taught from time to time at various universities, I've often relied on informal conversations with students to learn about their housing problems, preferences, likes, and dislikes. These conversations helped me develop my strategy for the 16-unit income property I mentioned previously.

How many people do you know (or know of) who have shopped to buy or rent housing in the past year or two? Talk with them. Learn their reactions to the properties they looked at. Why did they eventually choose their current home? What was the difference that made *the* difference for these people? What features would they have liked yet found rare or unavailable? Talk with people. Ask questions. You'll surprise yourself at how much valuable information you can pick up.

PAY ATTENTION

Read the neighborhood and community sections of the local newspaper(s). Follow those human interest stories and question-and-answer columns where people talk about their house-hunting and rental problems. Go to the library and read the articles in the Sunday Real Estate or Homes sections of *The Los Angeles Times, The San Diego Union-Tribune, The San Francisco Examiner, The Chicago Tribune, or The Orlando Sentinel,* or the Saturday edition of *The Washington Post.* These newspapers not only feature stories on the latest real estate trends but also carry the nationally syndicated columnists Robert Bruss, Kenneth Harney, and Lew Siechelman.

You can find other idea-provoking articles in magazines such as *American Demographics*, *Journal of Property Management*, and *Today's Realtor*. Eavesdrop. Turn your ears toward people when they talk about real estate. Visit real estate chat rooms on the Internet. When you discover something new or interesting, mull it over. Think whether this fact, trend, or problem could help you better tailor a property toward a market segment of renters (buyers). Is there some feature or benefit that you could offer that establishes a competitive advantage for your property or properties?

TALK WITH INSIDERS AND EXPERTS

A dozen or more occupations and professions exist where those employed gain firsthand, insider information by talking directly with home buyers and renters. Talk with people who work in these types of jobs:

- Real estate agents.
- Property managers.
- Mortgage loan reps.
- Property inspectors.
- Credit counselors.
- Remodeling contractors.
- Real estate investors.
- Newspaper reporters who cover housing and real estate.
- Existing tenants.
- Social service agency personnel.
- City planners, building permit inspectors, zoning personnel.
- Professors (architecture, consumer sciences, planning, real estate, housing).
- Staff who work at the city and state housing finance agencies.
- Apartment finder services.
- Roommate finder services.

- Code enforcers.
- Home builders.
- Government landlord/tenant agencies.
- HUD Section 8 administrators.

Discover demographic and psychographic trends, personal problems, shortages, and surpluses. Ask who's renting, who's buying, where, and why? What's hot, what's not? When home owners remodel, what features do they prefer? Are increasing (decreasing) numbers of people feeling financial pain? Trend analysis shows you how to profitably adapt to change.

FOCUS GROUPS

During the past 20 years, focus groups have emerged as one of the most popular ways to get into the minds of potential tenants and home buyers. Focus groups bring together 6 to 15 people from your proposed target market. Then, through give-and-take conversations, you probe their beliefs and feelings.

Most major home and apartment builders in the country now run focus groups to learn the preferences of their intended customers. To a certain degree, I ran my Stop Renting Now! seminars as quasi focus groups. Often real estate firms and mortgage lenders paid my fees. In return, I provided these clients the names of prospects along with the comments and concerns that I had elicited from my seminar's question-and-answer sessions.

In creating its share-a-home property, Tropical Village employed the Osceola County Council on Aging to hold 15 focus groups (200 total participants). The insights gained helped Tropical Village formulate its marketing theme as well as the specific features, amenities, and services that the firm blended into its triplexes and total value proposition.

To take advantage of this research technique, you need not conduct a formal focus group. That may go beyond the time, effort, and money that you want to put into your investment research—at least during your beginning stages. Nevertheless, if you find yourself (or can place yourself) in a group setting, try to get the group members to discuss topics that alert you to rental (sales) market opportunities. Scout for profitable ideas everywhere you can find them.

Anticipate and Adapt to Change

Anticipate change. Discover how trends will affect future demand for specific types of homes, apartments, neighborhoods, and communities. If you look at the writing on the wall, it reads, "Profit."

The Age Wave

Everybody knows that the population is getting older. During the next 20 years, 60 to 70 million people will celebrate their 60th birthday.[2] Sixty million new retirees are on the horizon. Where will these people want to live? What kinds of housing units will they want (share-a-homes)? What features amenities, services, and benefits will press their hot buttons?

The real estate investors who jump on the front end of this freight train to opportunity will certainly ride to glory. Yet, as I have emphasized, "over 60" itself doesn't define a target market per se. It merely flashes the signal to stop, look, and listen. What bull's-eye segments within this over-60 market will remain underserved until some entrepreneur senses their need and creates a way to fill it? Here are some of the trends that demographers are beginning to detect.

---

[2] The media frequently report a figure of around 75 million baby boomers. But that figure overstates the actual number because millions of boomers will die prior to age 60. However, we must add immigrants to the total number, thus the number is more than 60 million, but probably less than 70 million.

1. *Downsizing:* A shift away from the McMansions that became so popular during the late 1980s and 1990s.
2. *College Towns:* Retirees like the combination of education, sports, arts, theater, health facilities, and diversity without the big-city costs and aggravation.
3. *Rural/Small Towns:* Especially those towns that combine abundant outdoor recreation with a degree of upscale culture (such as Ashland, Oregon).
4. *Single-Floor Housing Units:* Post-60s often prefer to avoid stairs.
5. *Doorways and Door Levers:* Wider doorways to accommodate wheelchairs and walkers. Door levers are easier to manage than doorknobs.
6. *Mild Four-Season Climate:* While Florida will remain the most popular state for retirees, mild four-season states, such as Tennessee, Georgia, the Carolinas, Virginia, New Mexico, and Colorado, will become increasingly popular. In fact, the entire South will grow the number of migrant retirees.
7. *High-Cost to Low-Cost Areas:* Why live in a prewar Brooklyn bungalow when you can rent or own a large new house or apartment just outside sunny Orlando or Tampa for less than half the housing costs in Brooklyn?
8. *Security and Low Maintenance:* Lock and leave without worry. With extensive travel on the agenda, retirees won't want to concern themselves with the safety and security of their home while they're away.

These trends represent just a sampling of senior trends to be expected. Talk to the older people you know. What plans are they making? What features and benefits will motivate their next purchase or rental?

ECHO BOOMERS

Each year, thousands of articles discuss the effects that aging baby boomers will create for the housing market. To date, though, the media have not spent much time on another perfectly predictable demographic trend.

The birth years for baby boomers were from 1946 to 1964. The birth years for the baby bust were from 1965 to 1977. Then, beginning in 1978, annual births again started to climb into the range of 4 million per year and continued at or near that pace for more than 15 years.

The first of these echo boomers turned age 25 in 2003. Reminiscent of the 1970s, once again, near record numbers of young people will be flooding into the entry-level housing market. What types of apartments, what features, and what locations will appeal to the diverse segments of the echo generation? Put up your early detection antennae. What signals are the echo boomers sending as to how their preferences will evolve?

LOCAL TRENDS AND CHANGES

The age wave and the echo boomers represent two definite and profound demographic changes that will hit full stride during this decade. How will these trends impact the areas where you plan to invest? Or, vice versa, can you discover areas (neighborhoods, communities) that stand to benefit from the exploding growth of these two age-groups?

What other demographic and psychographic trends are occurring in your investment area? When you talk with housing experts and insiders, explore their views about population and community change. Track shifts in tastes, age distribution, incomes, job growth, and neighborhood popularity. Find a trend and ride it to profits.

As the trend grows, so will your knowledge and ability. You will learn from your tenants. You will refine and expand your property purchase, property improvement, and rental strategy. Your MVP will lead the curve.

8

Profit with and within the Rules

"The addition of this luxury structure to Jersey City's Gold Coast is a testament to the attraction of our city as a destination for people to live, work, and raise families. We are pleased to welcome Mr. Trump and Mr. Geibel as codevelopers of this project whose shared vision contributes to the continued growth and success of our downtown revitalization," said Jersey City's Mayor Jerramiah T. Healy.

"We are honored to be working with Donald Trump to create a world-class living experience in Jersey City, with its incomparable views of the world's most famous skyline, outstanding amenities, and convenient transportation links. I also want to thank Mayor Healy for his efforts to create an environment where Trump Plaza is possible," said Geibel, whose Hoboken-based Metro Homes LLC is the codeveloper of the project.

In Tampa, Florida, a newly announced Trump project gained similar acclaim. "This is an exciting development for Tampa, in many ways," said Mark Huey, the city's economic development administrator, on behalf of Mayor Pam Iorio. "When this project was announced last year, the focus and attention on the vibrancy and viability of downtown Tampa as a wonderful place to live, work, and play was taken to a new level. We're delighted with how Trump Tower Tampa incorporates and celebrates the Tampa Riverwalk and how this level of investment and commitment to quality reflects on our city."

"The entire development team is mindful of the significance and impact this project will have on the City of Tampa and the downtown area," stated Jill Cremer, vice president of development and marketing for The Trump Organization. "To that end, we took all the time and steps necessary to make sure that every aspect of this development would be executed to the highest standards which Mr. Trump and his partners at SimDag share."

What do both of these projects have in common? What do all Trump Organization projects have in common? The ability of the Trump team to work with government officials to secure zoning and building approvals.

Of course, when working with government, nothing is guaranteed. Mr. Trump's well-publicized battles with former New York City Mayor Ed Koch testify to that fact. Nevertheless, more than a small part of Mr. Trump's success lies in his ability to work the zoning and land-use laws to his benefit. When preparing to buy a site or building, Mr. Trump closely reviews all applicable building regulations as well as the sentiments of the city officials and community residents. In every case, he's trying to identify opportunities to use the property in a way that maximizes value.

Most famously, perhaps, was his coup to build 90 stories on a site originally zoned for less than half of that amount of space. The secret: buying up the air rights from the surrounding property owners—at the time a little recognized loophole in the zoning law. Today, Trump World Tower at United Nations Plaza stands as one of the tallest residential buildings in the world.

Use enthusiasm to capture and excite the people you need to get your deals permitted, financed, leased, and sold. Enthusiasm is contagious.

A FRIEND OF the curmudgeon 1930s actor W. C. Fields once spied Fields reading the Bible. "Bill," the friend said, "why are you reading the Bible? That doesn't seem like you." "Looking for loopholes," Fields answered, "looking for loopholes."

You need to read the rules, regulations, and laws that govern property and land use for the same reason that W. C. Fields read the Bible: to look for loopholes. As you craft your value proposition and MVP (most valued property) strategy, you will encounter a web of restrictions. The question then becomes, Will you get stuck and entangled within this web? Or, like the agile spider, will you learn to use this web to benefit you and your market segment of tenants or buyers?

Without the agility to navigate this web of rules, you can make these mistakes:

1. *Missed Advantages:* You will renovate, manage, rent, and sell your properties to create your MVP. Yet without detailed knowledge of what you can and cannot legally do, you can miss profitable possibilities. Or you might assume incorrectly that you can make some changes in property features or use that current laws prohibit.
2. *Purchase Errors:* Prior to purchase, learn whether the property stands within all applicable laws. Otherwise, the regulators might require you to make costly renovations to modify the property to conform to code. If that enclosed porch or converted attic doesn't fit within the regulations, you may have to tear out these illegal improvements and rebuild according to code.
3. *Mistakes in Use:* Land-use rules create zoning districts (commercial, residential, industrial), and they also govern occupancy, signs, parking, home businesses, noise, yard care, and even whether you can put up a basketball hoop or hang clothes on an outdoor clothesline.
4. *Mismanagement of Rentals:* Federal, state, and local laws govern every issue from security deposits to discrimination to eviction. Failure to follow lawful rules and procedures can subject you to fines or liability claims and court judgments.

To profit with property, follow the rules, change the rules, or seek a lawful exception. I've heard investors rail against the rules of government or the rules of their homeowners' associations. Yet these rules were in effect at the time the investors bought. These disgruntled folks had failed to investigate before they invested.

To profit with property, study the government, private, and contractual rules that govern your property (or the property that you're evaluating to buy). Your superior knowledge will pay off in two ways: (1) You will capitalize on profitable opportunities that others miss, and (2) you will steer around those entanglements that ensnare others. Here are the main sources of laws that govern your properties:

- Homeowners' associations.
- Private contracts, such as mortgages, leases, insurance policies, and easements.
- Governments (federal, state, county, city).

Restrictions, of course, do not govern only *your* property. They govern that of your neighbors and your tenants. You can use the rules to stop others from acting in ways that run down the value of your property. For example, use the rules to control the neighborhood riffraff or to straighten up troublesome tenants.

Condo, Co-Op, and Subdivision Associations

In addition to city, state, and federal governments, private governments now issue rules, regulations, and laws that courts will enforce. These private governments also tax, assess, fine, and collect fees from their citizens. As with rules and regulations, courts will enforce payment of these charges. Absent payment, these private governments can foreclose on their delinquent property owners.

What private governments exercise such authority and powers? Condo, co-op, and subdivision associations. Today, more than 35 percent of all homes in the United States and Canada are ruled by some type of homeowners' associations (HOAs). Although generally HOAs perform reasonably well, never assume that peace, responsibility, and fiscal discipline prevail within such a community of owners and residents.

Obtain a Copy of the Resale Package

Before you invest in a property that's governed by an HOA, obtain and closely read a copy of its so-called resale package. This package provides the HOA's constitution, bylaws (declarations), rules and regulations, budget, reserves for repairs and replacement, and other operating policies and procedures.

As you read through a copy of these documents, verify that the law of the complex will permit you carry out the entrepreneurial strategy that you would like to execute for the property. In addition, figure out the amount of fees, assessments, and maintenance charges that the HOA will require you to pay.

Types of Rules and Regulations

Some HOAs tread lightly. Others detail conduct, property upkeep, property improvements, and occupancy in such a minute manner only a diehard communist could tolerate. The HOA can govern parking, music, cooking, grilling, moving in, moving out, lease terms, pets, and the types, numbers, and ages of tenants—plus virtually anything else you can think of.

I stress this "need to know" about the HOA because I see many investors buy properties and then learn they can't renovate or lease out their units as they intended. Or they're hit with large unanticipated fees or assessments. (In this book, we can't go into detail about HOAs, but my book *Make Money with Condominiums and Townhouses* thoroughly addresses all of these topics.)

CONTRACTS RESTRICT PROPERTY USE AND IMPROVEMENTS

You realize that HOAs, as well as local, state, and federal governments, can limit your right to do with your property as you please. But did you know that mortgage and insurance contracts also set forth rules and restrictions?

For example, mortgage contracts often include clauses that require you to do the following:

1. Maintain the property in good repair.
2. Obtain the lender's written permission before remodeling or making other substantive changes to the property.

3. Obtain the lender's written permission before you change the use of the property (converting it, say, from residential to office or retail). Usually, you will need to arrange new financing.
4. Live in the property for at least 12 months—unless you've financed it with higher-cost investor (non–owner occupied) financing.

Similarly, your property insurance policy will include clauses that apply to use, occupancy, vacancies, materials and repairs, and major renovations. If you materially breach the mortgage agreement, the lender can (after notice to cure) call the loan due immediately. If you materially breach the insurance agreement, the insurer may refuse to pay any claim you file. Play it safe. Before you risk a violation, read your mortgage loan and insurance contracts.

Zoning and Related Ordinances

Since the 1920s, zoning and other property ordinances have steadily increased their coverage. To learn how zoning affects a property, consult your area's zoning map. Find out the type of zoning district and the relevant governing rules and regulations. Or locate those neighborhoods that are zoned appropriately. Then look for properties that will legally fit within your entrepreneurial plans. Zoning laws tailor specific rules to specific districts.

The District Concept

To set up zoning laws, planners design zoning maps that lay out multiple districts that may range in size from one small parcel of land up to several square miles or more. Sometimes, small zoning districts lie within larger districts—as when a small office complex or convenience retail center is surrounded by residences. Elite cities may even zone the entire community all one district (typically, single-family residential).

As you can see from Figure 8.1, planners have invented all kinds of zoning districts. This listing in Figure 8.1 samples only a few district categories. A full listing of categories could number into the hundreds.

If a property, for example, were located in a city's RMU (residential mixed use) district, you would turn to Section 30-54 of the city's zoning manual. If from the zoning map you see that the property is located in a RSF-4 district, you would consult Section 30-51. From the zoning manual, you would learn the specific rules that govern properties located within the applicable district category.

What Kinds of Restrictions?

As Table 8.1 shows, zoning and other related ordinances can control about anything you do outside the privacy of your own bedroom. Some cities (such as Palm Beach, Florida, or Mill Valley, California [Marin County]) regulate everything that's possible as tightly as possible. Other cities (such as Orlando, Florida) adopt a more liberal policy. In Gilcrest County, Florida, it appears as if anyone can place a mobile home about anywhere without fear of legal challenge. In the next county of Alachua, legal sites for mobile homes are tough to come by. With some governments, almost "anything goes." With others, you need permission to put up a new mailbox.

Setbacks, Side Yards, and Height

Zoning ordinances tell property owners that they can't site their buildings too close to the street, their adjacent neighbors, or the neighboring site in the rear. What's too close? What buildings? It all depends.

1. *Dimensions:* Look at Table 8.2. You can see the requirements for four different residential single-family (RSF) classifications in one small town. Except for the maximum height requirements of 35 feet, the other dimensional standards *do not* represent "typical." In fact, no typical exists. Until the

---

Article IV. Use Regulations

Division 1. Introduction to Districts

Sec. 30-41.   Establishment of zoning districts and categories
Sec. 30-42.   Designation of district boundaries
Sec. 30-43.   Rules for interpretation of district boundaries

Residential Zoning Districts

Sec. 30-51.   Single-family residential districts (RSF-1, RSF-2, RSF-2 and RSF-4)
Sec. 30-52.   Residential low-density districts (RMF-5, RC and MH)
Sec. 30-53.   Multiple-family medium-density residential districts (RMF-6, RMF-7, and RMF-8)
Sec. 30-54.   Residential mixed-use district (RMU)
Sec. 30-55.   Residential high-density districts (RH-1 and RH-2)
Sec. 30-56.   General provisions for residential districts
Sec. 30-57.   Residential leases; teaching of the fine arts
Sec. 30-58.   Home occupation permits

Office Zoning Districts

Sec. 30-59.   Office districts (OR and OF)
Sec. 30-60.   General provisions for office districts

Business and Mixed-Use Zoning Districts

Sec. 30-61.   General business district (BUS)
Sec. 30-62.   Automotive-oriented business district (BA)
Sec. 30-63.   Tourist-oriented business district (BT)
Sec. 30-64.   Mixed-use low-intensity district (MU-1)
Sec. 30-65.   Mixed-use medium-intensity district (MU-2)
Sec. 30-66.   Central city district (CCD)
Sec. 30-67.   General provisions for business and mixed-use districts

---

Figure 8.1   Common Types of Zoning Districts.

zoning law was recently changed, Vancouver, British Columbia, permitted some RSFs with a lot width of 16 feet, side yards of two feet, and front setbacks of 10 feet. In Barrington Hills, an exclusive suburb of Chicago, minimum lot sizes require five acres. Some planned unit developments permit zero lot lines, as do some big-city townhouses and tenements. (Note: The du/a shorthand in Table 8.2 stands for dwelling units per acre.)

Table 8.1 A Sampling of Concerns for Zoning and Other Related Ordinances

Type of property use
Special uses/exceptions
Setback dimensions (front and rear)
Side-yard dimensions
Floor area ratio (FAR)
Lot coverage ratio
Building height
Parking
Noise
Light
View
Trees and shrubbery
Accessory apartments
Swimming pools
Subdivision layout
Animal control
Party walls
Obnoxious behavior
Smoke, dust, pollution
Aesthetics/Architectural Review Boards
Occupancy
Home occupations
Home businesses
Trespass
Fences
Crowds
Historical districts
Yard care, weeds
Health and safety
Solar panels
Signage
Environment and ecology

2. *Buildings or Structures:* When you check the requirements for setbacks and side yards, notice what buildings or structures must comply. Zoning rules may permit screened porches, freestanding storage sheds, swimming pools,

Table 8.2 Dimensional Requirements for Residential Single-Family (RSF) Districts

Principal Structures	RSF-1	RSF-2	RSF-3	RSF-4
Maximum density	3.5 du/a	4.6 du/a	5.8 du/a	8 du/a
Minimum lot area	8,500 sq. ft.	7,500 sq. ft.	6,000 sq. ft.	4,300 sq. ft.
Minimum lot width at minimum front-yard setback	85 ft.	75 ft.	60 ft.	50 ft.
Minimum lot depth	90 ft.	90 ft.	90 ft.	80 ft.
Minimum yard setbacks				
Front	20 ft.	20 ft.	20 ft.	20 ft.
Side (interior)	7.5 ft.	7.5 ft.	7.5 ft.	7.5 ft.
Side (street)	10 ft.	10 ft.	7.5 ft.	7.5 ft.
Rear	20 ft.	20 ft.	15 ft.	10 ft.
Maximum building height	35 ft.	35 ft.	35 ft.	35 ft.
Accessory Structures,[1] Excluding Fences and Walls				
Minimum front- and side-yard setbacks	Same requirements are for the principal structure			
Minimum yard setback, rear[2]	7.5 ft.			
Maximum building height	25 ft.			
Transmitter towers	80 ft.			

[1] Accessory screened enclosure structures, whether or not attached to the principal structure, may be erected in the rear yard as long as the enclosure has a minimum yard setback of three feet from the rear property line. The maximum height of the enclosure at the setback line shall not exceed eight feet. The roof and all sides of the enclosure not attached to the principal structure must be made of screening material.

[2] One preengineered or premanufactured structure of 100 square feet or less may be erected in the rear and side yards as long as the structure has a minimum yard setback of three feet from the rear or side property lines, is properly anchored to the ground, and is separated from neighboring properties by a fence or wall that is at least 75 percent opaque.

decks, garages, and driveways to sit closer to the property lines. With such exceptions common, you may enjoy more room for improvements than a casual glance at the requirements might imply. Setbacks do not necessarily apply to all types of structures and improvements.

Floor Area and Lot Coverage Ratios

If you plan to add living or storage space to the main structure, check to see whether the zoning code sets floor area (FARs) or lot coverage ratios (LCRs) for the property. An FAR expresses the square footage of the structure as a percentage of the square footage of the lot:

$$\text{Floor area ratio (FAR)} = \frac{2{,}400 \text{ sq. ft. (building size)}}{8{,}500 \text{ sq. ft. (lot size)}}$$

$$\text{FAR} = 28.2\%$$

If a regulation limited the FAR to, say, 35 percent, you could add up to 575 square feet of building size:

$$\text{Maximum FAR} = .35 \times 8{,}500$$
$$= 2{,}975 \text{ sq. ft.}$$

However, your plans also might have to fit within an LCR. To leave enough room for parking and yard space, site planners may limit the footprint of the building to some specified percentage of the site size. Say, in the previous example, that zoning set the maximum LCR at 30 percent. You would have to add your space into a second story rather than build a ground-floor addition:

$$30\% \text{ (LCR maximum)} \times 8{,}500 \text{ sq. ft. (lot size)}$$
$$= 2{,}550 \text{ sq. ft. (maximum footprint)}$$

Now another complicating issue. What parts of the structure count in these ratios? Basements, decks, porches, garages, driveways? There's only one way to find out. Read the zoning ordinance. If the ordinance remains silent or seems ambiguous, talk with a land-use lawyer to see whether you might have found a profitable loophole.

Occupancy Restrictions

I recently inquired about a single-family investment property that was up for sale. The seller told me that the house was rented to five college students for $1,500 a month. "Sounds pretty good," I said. Then, hoping to win some negotiating points, I mentioned that the city's occupancy code limited single-family rentals to three unrelated adults. Therefore, I couldn't pay what the seller was asking because I would risk a code enforcement that would cost my rental income.

"No problem," the seller countered. "This house sits in a commercial district. Five students don't violate the commercial district code."

Well, he had me. It turns out that, on this issue, he knew more about the code than I did—at least as it applied to his property. Smart seller. He had anticipated code questions and had prepared factual and accurate responses. A refreshing change from most run-of-the-mill sellers and real estate agents who don't bother to learn anything about the land-use codes—until a serious mistake teaches them a hard lesson.

Never assume that you know the zoning law. Quirks and loopholes run everywhere.

Parking

"No on-street parking between the hours of 2:00 a.m. and 6:00 a.m." You might think that neighborhood parking ordinances relate to traffic issues. Sometimes they do. But sometimes restricted parking hours indirectly control the population density of a neighborhood. How can 8, 10, or 15 occupants of a single-family house find adequate on-site parking? Park in the front yard? The zoning (or other) rules probably outlaw that response because they typically regulate all types of on-street and off-street parking.

Home Businesses/Home Occupations

Millions of people now work out of their homes. This trend will continue to grow. Renovating and remodeling houses to meet this home office need can present an entrepreneurial opportunity. But beware: Zoning rules closely regulate people who want to operate an office or run a business from their residence. (HOAs frequently impose even stricter home business rules than zoning laws.)

Questions to Answer. Does the zoning district of the property permit work at home as a right? If not, can you fit within a special exception category (see later discussion)? What rules apply to parking, the number of allowable customer visits, hours of operation, signage, business licenses, and dedicated space? To what extent could you legally modify the structure to accommodate the home office or business? Can you rent the office or business portion of the residence to someone who doesn't live there? Precisely what types of occupations or businesses will zoning permit?

Missed Opportunity. A majority of investors miss this market. Depending on the wording of the ordinance, you could target any of the following:

- Writers.
- Artists.
- Accountants.
- Lawyers.
- Insurance agents.
- Music instruction.
- Financial planner.
- Seamstress/tailor.
- Beauty shop.
- Network marketers.
- Child care.
- Answering service.

This list merely samples the unlimited variety of small, independent occupations and businesses that proliferate in our rapidly evolving free-agent nation where many people can live wherever they choose to live. Learn what locations and what property features work best for one or more types of these free agents, and you may find a lucrative niche of entrepreneurial opportunity.

Special Uses

Typically, zoning districts permit certain uses as rights and other named uses as special exceptions. If designated a right, you can proceed with your plans without delay. As long as you comply with setbacks, height, and other details, zoning administrators must approve your intentions (unless they find a loophole of their own to use against *you*—or your plans). If the use is classified within the special exception category, zoning officials could deny (or modify) your plans (see Table 8.3). To do so properly, they would have to object because your use would harm the public interest or create adverse effects for neighboring property owners. Fortunately, you can challenge the planner's objection. And if you end up in court, the judge will reverse the normal legal presumption that planners know best. Instead, the planners must prove through the greater weight of the evidence that their opinion should rule.

Do not assume that a residential, commercial, or industrial district necessarily excludes other uses. Even districts zoned single family typically permit other types of property uses.

Noise Ordinances

In most communities, noise ordinances restrict the maximum decibel levels that are tolerated within various zoning districts. If a noisy neighbor makes it difficult for you to sell or rent one of your properties, don't fight a neighbor war. Instead, insist that the code enforcer emphatically tell the offender to cease and desist. Likewise, if your tenants party into the wee hours and create neighborhood revolt, use the law to stifle their boisterous behavior.

Table 8.3 Uses by Right or Special Exception as per One City Zoning Ordinance for a Single-Family District (R-1-AA)

District: Single-Family (R-1-AA)	
Uses by Right	Uses by Special Exception
1. Single-family houses	1. Public or private schools
2. Customary accessory uses	2. In-home professional offices
3. Boathouses and boat docks	3. Churches
4. Foster homes	4. Tennis clubs
5. Adult congregate living facilities	5. Guest cottages
	6. Golf courses
	7. Public swimming pools
	8. Shelter homes

How to Challenge the Zoning Rules

If you feel that zoning rules impact your property too harshly, seek change or attack the zoning law itself. You can pursue a remedy in some combination of the following:

- Seek a variance.
- Petition for rezoning.
- Go to court.

Emphasize on telling people how they'd benefit if they go through with the deal.

Seek a Variance

As a matter of right, property owners may request a variance when a zoning rule creates undue hardship. Typically, "I want to make more money" doesn't qualify as hardship. From the planner's perspective, that "hardship" qualifies as tough luck.

When planners speak of hardship, they mean some unique feature of your property that renders it difficult to use in what would otherwise be a legal manner. Say that side-yard setbacks require 10 feet. Your lot line cuts at an angle. At the front part of your planned addition, you've got 12 feet of width, but at the back part, only 8 feet of width. Absent some serious objection by the adjacent property owner, you would probably get your variance.

If the critics or the press harass you, turn their negatives into positives. "The building's too tall." "Doesn't New York deserve the world's tallest building?"

Petition for Rezoning

If your property is uniquely situated to benefit from a more profitable use, petition the planners to rezone your site. Say that because of a new nearby office development, increased traffic flows, and the evolving nature of the neighborhood, you could propose that your building deserves another zoning classification. Professional offices would now better fit this location.

When you work with the land-use and zoning personnel, wear kid gloves and handle with care. Unless all else fails, don't try to bulldoze your way through permissions. Human and political relations count as much as the rules and regulations that fill their manuals.

Unlike a variance, which according to contemporary zoning theory should require only adjusting a regulatory detail or two, rezoning puts you in another league with a new set of rules. As with a variance, planners won't rezone your property (or the neighborhood) unless you show that rezoning will not harm contiguous properties or the integrity of the overall community plan.

Go to Court

Nearly all zoning laws give property owners and citizens several levels of appeal within the system. If you strike out with frontline personnel, next go to the department head, then to a zoning board of adjustment, and eventually perhaps to a city or county council. Should you fail at these levels, you alone (or with other property owners who endorse the change) can file suit.

Typically, you might sue to force government to treat you and your property in a way that better serves your interests. Or you might sue to block the rezoning or planned use of nearby land that will bear adversely on the value of your property as well as the health, safety, morals, or general welfare of the community. (Remember, whenever possible, work the community-needs angle into your argument. Ayn Rand notwithstanding, neither planners nor judges typically appreciate the virtue of pure selfishness. Position your request in terms of the public interest.)

BUILDING CODES

We haven't yet distinguished zoning and other types of land-use codes from building codes. Partly that's because no clear distinction applies. A rule that falls under zoning in one locale may fall under the building codes in another. Sometimes controls overlap.

For your purposes, you will meet up primarily with *building code* inspectors when you perform (or contract for) major plumbing, electrical, remodeling, or roofing work. These building codes may force you to use construction techniques, design, or materials that can add to your costs (generally for reasons of safety). But they will seldom seriously restrict basic plans for renovation and market strategy (as can zoning and other land-use ordinances). Remember, too, that if you do your own work, your work still must comply with permits and codes.

Environmental Laws

Property investors may run into five types of environmental issues:

- Lead paint.
- Asbestos.
- Underground home heating oil tanks (especially if one has been leaking).
- Septic systems and wastewater disposal.
- Tree ordinances.

Let's deal with the easiest first. Tree ordinances may prohibit you from cutting down a tree on your property. This could make a room addition more difficult or impossible. Or maybe you want to destroy the tree to enhance a view of the mountains or bay. Views may add more value than the tree, but the tree law could block you from achieving that gain.

As to the costly issues of lead paint, asbestos, heating oil tanks, and waste disposal (if the property's not connected to a city or county sewer line), get copies of the pertinent brochures published by local, state, and federal environmental agencies. If you find a property that requires abatement of any of these problems (unless you have deep pockets and the property shows great potential), get back into your car and look for another investment.

Beginning investors should not carry out an environmental cleanup. Too much risk for too little payback. Instead, focus on value-enhancing opportunities to create your MVP. It's to that topic that we now turn.

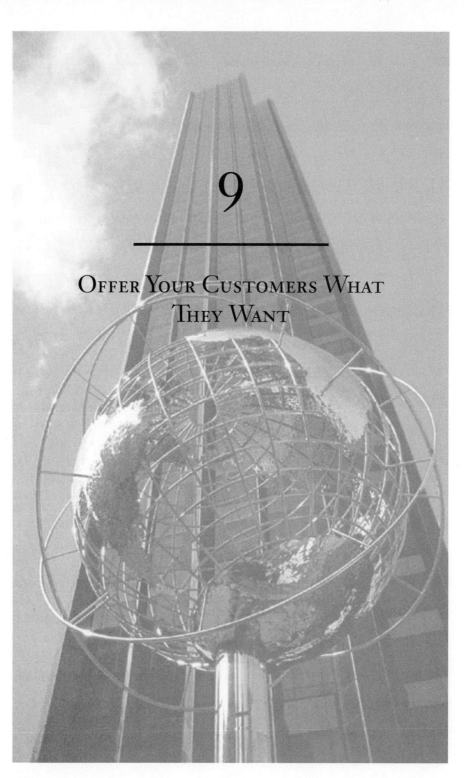

9

OFFER YOUR CUSTOMERS WHAT THEY WANT

Give Your Customers
What They Want

Today, the public knows Donald Trump as a builder who offers his super wealthy customers the best of breed in luxury hotels, condominiums, golf courses, and retail stores. But most people do not realize that his early real estate experiences focused on homebuyers and tenants whose income and wealth (if any) placed them further down the demographic ladder. Nevertheless, even with these humble market segments, Mr. Trump still ranked supreme the foundation principle, "Give your customers what they want." And so should you.

Consider Swifton Village. While in college, Mr. Trump thought and read about real estate more than he followed sports or planned wild fraternity parties. That's when he discovered Swifton Village. As he was reading the Federal Housing Administration's (FHA) list of fore-closed apartment buildings,[1] he spied this deeply troubled, 1,200-unit property. Always alert to opportunity, Mr. Trump investigated further.

He learned that the FHA badly wanted to rid itself of this property that was then nearly 70 percent vacant. With this knowledge, Donald and his father negotiated a sweet deal and arranged some favorable financing.

Nevertheless, no matter how sweet the deal and how juicy the financing, you can't profitably operate a rental property that fails to attract good rent-paying tenants. And to attract and retain good rent-paying tenants, you must offer tenants something better than your competitors (remember the MVP goal). To achieve this objective, the Trump team (among other things), created a new set of features and benefits:

1. Eliminated bad tenants. Bad tenants drive out good tenants. If you don't quickly deal with problem tenants (or the problems that tenants present), you'll soon find that your entire property has turned into a money pit of vacancies and repairs.

---

[1] You can find these foreclosures today at fha.gov.

2. Beefed up safety and security. It's not just the rich who care about safety and security, all decent people want to live free of hooligans and drug dealers. The Trump team initiated safety and security measures that included a grounds patrol.

3. Improved the aesthetics. Good tenants want to live in a home that shows pride of ownership. When serving the less well off, many property owners forget this fact. Mr. Trump thought differently. So, he attended to not just big ticket maintenance issues. He also cared enough to add special homey touches such as white shutters, colonial white doors (to replace the ugly, cheap aluminum doors), and an impeccable cleaning program.

Know your customers. You've got to really get into the mind of the audience you're aiming at. I don't like hired gun, number-crunching market researchers. I do my own surveys and research. I draw my own conclusions.

GOVERNMENT, HOMEOWNERS' ASSOCIATIONS, AND contracts set the rules for property use and improvements. Within those rules, you are free to design your entrepreneurial MVP (most valued property) strategy to give your targeted customers what they want—and what they're willing to pay for. From your customers' viewpoint, the MVP favorably distinguishes your property from competing properties. From your perspective, the MVP adds to your cash flows and equity buildup. You achieve the ideal match: a win-win outcome.

SEARCH FOR COMPETITIVE ADVANTAGE (CREATE YOUR MVP)

Many owners of investment properties still think of themselves as "landlords" (with an emphasis on "m' lord"), and they think of their residents merely as "renters" who don't deserve customer care. But just the opposite is true. Today (and in the future), market conditions require savvy investors to treat their tenants as valued customers—not serfs.

I don't just build to a market. I create the market. I deliver to my customers more than they expect.

To create an MVP, intelligently survey and inspect competing properties. This market knowledge helps give you the insight you need to strategically customize your properties to make them stand out from competitors. When you adopt this MVP approach, you add to your profits (and to the value of your properties) for two reasons:

1. *Better Resident Relations:* The residents of your properties will reward you with lower turnover, fewer problems, and higher rents.
2. *Alert to Opportunities:* With a customer-oriented, constant-improvement attitude, you will consistently look for and come up with ideas that will add value to your property operations.

INVENTORY COMPETITORS

If houses and apartments were like cans of Campbell's tomato soup or bottles of Coca-Cola, every similar-sized unit would rent (or sell) for the same price. You could discover an actual "market" rent or price level. But houses and apartments aren't cans of soup. They differ in dozens of ways that potential tenants (buyers) find appealing or unappealing.

You can create a prestige effect with any property. Just make it the best of breed for your market segment.

You can use any (some, all) of these differences to set your property apart from the crowd. When you tour competing properties, what do you see? How do the properties rate with respect to the following features?

- Views.
- Energy usage/efficiency.
- Square footage (rentable, usable).
- Natural light.
- Ceiling height.
- Quiet/noisiness.
- Parking.
- Room count.
- Appliances (quality, quantity).
- Landscaping.
- Quality of finishes.
- Heat/air-conditioning.
- Decks/patios/balconies.
- Cleanliness.
- Carpeting/floor coverings.
- Electrical outlets.
- Emotional appeal.
- Color schemes/aesthetics.
- Living area floor plan.
- Closet space.
- Storage space.
- Kitchen functionality.
- Entryway convenience.
- Tenant demographics.
- Tenant lifestyles, attitudes.
- Lighting.
- Security.
- Laundry facilities.
- Fireplace.
- Physical condition.
- Window coverings.
- Types/style of windows.
- Image/reputation.
- Furniture.
- Kitchen pizzazz.

This checklist doesn't mention other important tenant concerns, such as the amount of the security deposit (total move-in cash), the terms of the lease, the quality of the management, and, last but far from least, location. Unless you think through all of these possible differences, you can't intelligently say that your two-bedroom, two-bath units should rent for $975 a month. So compare and contrast your (prospective) property feature by feature to a selection of competing properties. Record every detail.

With accurate, firsthand information about competing property features and rent levels, you not only improve your ability to evaluate your property but also prime your mind to spot opportunities to increase its value.

Give Your Property a Donald Trump Makeover

After you have inventoried and inspected your competitors, go through your (prospective) property. Stimulate your thinking with the facts and ideas you found on your competitive tour. Here are some suggested ways to create an MVP. But in practice, your improvements should flow from both the tenant (buyer) preferences you've discovered and the quality of the competing properties.

We're spending $250 million on the building but taking nothing for granted. Every detail from marble patterns to the color of the window frames has got to work together to create the effect we want to achieve.

What's Your Overall Impression?

As you first walk into the unit, are you met with a bland neutrality? Do you see faded paint, scuff marks, outdated color schemes, cheap hollow-core doors, nail holes in the walls, worn carpeting, torn linoleum, old-fashioned light fixtures, cracked wall switch plates, or stained sinks? If you answer yes to any or all of these questions, you've found an easy way to create value.

Pay Special Attention to Kitchens and Baths

To really wow your potential tenants, bring in the Trump design team to redo the kitchens and bathrooms. Flip through the pages of those many kitchen and bath magazines. Look for that right combination of materials and colors that will create a light, bright, cheerful, and inviting look. Eliminate those harvest gold appliances, the chipped and stained sinks, and that cracked glass in the shower door. You don't typically need granite countertops, but you do need to create a "wow, isn't this beautiful" response.

As you inspect these key rooms, focus for at least 30 seconds on each of the following:

- Floors.
- Ceilings.
- Sinks.
- Toilet bowl.
- Windows and windowsills.
- Electrical outlet plates.
- Lighting.
- Faucets.
- Walls.
- Cabinets.
- Cabinet and drawer handles.
- Appliances.
- Countertops.
- Mirrors.

When you focus for 30 seconds on each detail in these rooms, you should notice any blemishes, cracks, stains, and so on that reflect unfavorably on the overall appeal. Focus leads you to see shortcomings that you would otherwise miss. Throughout the entire apartment (or house), all details count. But they especially count in the kitchens and baths. Add the right pizzazz to the kitchens and bathrooms, and you transform a ho-hum unit into a showplace.

Cleanliness Generates Profits

Do you want to attract tenants who will care for your properties? Thoroughly clean the units as if you are the hired property manager and Donald Trump is about to perform a white-glove inspection. Do not think "rental property." Think "home." Clean units attract clean tenants.

Clean everywhere. Remove the dirt, dust, cobwebs, and dead bugs from all corners, baseboards, light fixtures, and shelving. Pull out all kitchen drawers. Dump the bread crumbs and accumulated debris. Wipe all windows and mirrors to sparkle and shine. Look closely for grime and mold in the shower and shower door tracks. Scrape the rust out of the medicine cabinets and repaint where necessary. Eliminate all odors—the unit should not only look but also smell fresh and clean.

Natural Light and Views

If your units seem dark, brighten them up. Add bright colors, windows, or skylights. Remove light-blocking window coverings. If you're lucky, you might buy one of those older buildings with 10-foot ceilings—now artificially reduced to 8 feet via suspended acoustical tile. For a reason unknown to me (energy conservation?), dropped ceilings became popular in the 1960s and 1970s. Today, they're outdated. Rip them out. The rooms will seem larger and brighter. In rooms with high ceilings, install clerestory windows to bring in more light.

> **Add a view, add value. We built Trump tower with a spectacular design to give commanding views that gave us commanding power to sell apartments at prices that towered over competitors.**

For first-floor units, enhance the view with landscape or fencing. To create views for upper-story units, think long term. Plant trees. Although windows are expensive, weigh the costs and benefits of adding them. Ugly views turn off most tenants and buyers. Pleasant views provide good selling points. Give your tenants better views than dumpsters, parking lots, and the rooftops of other buildings. In return, they will pay you more in rent (or purchase price).

Special Touches

For those special aesthetic touches, accent with chair railings, wallpaper borders, upgraded door handles, paneled doors, and wood stains (rather than paint). Upgraded light fixtures, too, can help you add pizzazz. The newer track lighting systems have gained popularity with some market segments.

I always include special, unique features that dazzle my tenants or buyers and arouse their emotions.

Develop ideas for special touches from home decorating and remodeling magazines. Visit model homes and upscale apartment, townhouse, and condominium developments. Don't get carried away with special touches, or you will cut into your profitability. Still, a few "wow, look at this" features will help prospects differentiate and remember your units.

Safety, Security, and Convenience

Look for ways to combine safety and convenience. Increase the number and capacity of electrical outlets. Older buildings, especially, lack outlets and amperage to safely handle plug-in appliances, computers, printers, fax machines, and home entertainment centers. Many renters don't notice this functional obsolescence until after they move into a unit. Then they "solve" the problem with adapter plugs and roaming extension cords. If the unit lacks electrical capacity, plan an upgrade.

Peepholes for entry doors also match up security with convenience. Many people like to learn who's there before they open their door.

Other Issues of Safety and Security

Other safety issues of concern include smoke alarms, carbon monoxide detectors, fire escape routes, door locks, first-floor windows, and first-floor sliding glass doors. As security against break-ins, verify that all windows and doors lock tightly and cannot be jimmied with a credit card or even a screwdriver. Double-deadbolt locks are best.

Tenants and buyers want to feel safe in their homes. If doors, door locks, and windows seem flimsy or easily breached, some tenants won't rent the unit—regardless of its other oohs and aahs.

Environmental health hazards may exist because of lead paint, asbestos, or formaldehyde—any of which may be found in building materials used in construction (or remodeling) prior to 1978. Before you invest, obtain and review seller disclosures about these hazards. If the building is suspect, don't buy it without firm remedial cost figures from an abatement contractor.

Stairs, Carpets, and Bathrooms

Repair steps or stair railings that may be loose or dangerous. Frayed carpets and bathtubs that lack no-slip bottoms and handrails can result in falls. Itemize and remedy each safety and security hazard within the property. Even when a repair doesn't add to your rent collections, it protects your tenants. It reduces the chance that you could end up on the wrong end of a tenant's lawsuit for damages. Unsafe conditions and features provide evidence of negligence— mostly civil but sometimes criminal.

Rightsize the Rooms

Have you ever walked into a house or apartment and found some rooms too large, others too small? In many houses, builders design a huge great room along with a huge master bedroom and bath. Then they add three or four dink-sized bedrooms for kids, guests, or study. The house lacks a sense of proportion.

Create a Sense of Proportion

What "sense of proportion" should a house or an apartment unit display? The answer varies by tenant segment, price range, and timing. From decade to decade, tastes and preferences change. In turn, these changes present entrepreneurial opportunities for improvement. Buy an out-of-style building. Then redesign the internal floor plan to appeal to a contemporary market segment of renters or buyers.

Postwar Units Are Modernized

I once bought an eight-unit apartment building. It had been built in the late 1940s to meet the pressing demand for housing by returning veterans of World War II. The units still retained the three-bedroom, one-bath floor plan (common to that period)—one moderate-sized bedroom for the parents and two small bedrooms for those recently born baby boomers. In the early 1990s (when I bought the property), most tenants I wanted looked at the units and said, "Ugh, no way. We couldn't live here."

Because the seller had trouble keeping the units rented, I got a bargain price. To create value, I split one of the small bedrooms. I used half that space to enlarge the other small bedroom and the other half to add a second bathroom. I then rented the building to tenants looking to share their rentals with a roommate. Rent collections jumped by $175 per unit per month—a profitable return on my investment and renovations. The MVP strategy worked.

Create More Storage

Self-storage (miniwarehouses) represents one of the fastest-growing property uses in the United States and Europe. We've all become pack rats. "Throw it away? I might need that sometime." Talk with tenants. Talk with home owners. Many will tell you the same thing: "I like my home, but we lack space for storage." To add appeal to your rental houses and apartments, add storage space. You can add storage space in two basic ways:

- Bring dead space to life.
- Increase the usefulness of existing space.

Bring Dead Space to Life

Here's an example that may seem trivial, yet it mildly impresses prospective tenants. Look in the cabinet under your kitchen sink. You will see a small gap between the front panel of the cabinet above the door and the sink: dead space. How might you convert that small gap to usable space? Install a small pull-down compartment to stow away soap, sponge, and steel-wool pads. Eliminate sink clutter. Show this little innovation, and you'll receive a favorable response, such as, "Isn't that neat?"

Trivial? Maybe. Still, it illustrates the point. All houses and apartments include opportunistic quantities of dead space that you can bring to life:

- Under stairs and stairwells.
- Bay windows with storage built under the window seat and under the outside the window.
- Garden windows.
- On top of kitchen cabinets.
- Dead-end cabinets.
- Walls suitable for shelving.

- Recessed storage between studs (as with an in-wall medicine chest).
- Kitchen hanging bars for pots and pans.

Such ideas only sample the possibilities. If you search through any house or apartment and persistently ask, "Where are the dead spaces that I can bring to life for storage?" you will find them.

Increase the Usefulness of Existing Space

To achieve "more with less," follow the lead of the California Closet Company (CCC). As ideas from this innovative firm have proven, you can double (or triple) your storage capacity without adding one square inch of new space. Redesign space that already exists. Although founded as a closet company, CCC now redesigns basements, garages, offices, workshops, and kitchens. Put these same organizing principles to work, and you'll wow your prospects. You will offer a sought-after yet relatively scarce benefit.

In addition, multipurpose some space. For example, install a Murphy bed that folds up against (or into) a wall. A Murphy bed not only adds usable floor space but also creates possibilities for shelving alongside the bed. Use the existing wall cavity or create a larger cavity by bringing a new wall out even with the Murphy bed. Thoroughly inspect and note each opportunity a property offers to use space more effectively—both for storage and livability.

Abate Noise

No one likes noise. Before you invest, test the units for soundproofing. Will noise from a television or stereo carry throughout the house or apartment? When you inspect properties, bring along a portable radio. Test various rooms. Turn up the volume. Do the walls provide enough soundproofing? Families and roommate tenants want privacy and quiet. If your property fails to offer quiet, your units will lose appeal.

Check for Neighborhood Noise

Just as important, will your tenants (buyers) hear neighbors or neighborhood noise from inside their units? People pay for quiet. They heavily discount for noise.

You'll typically hear more noise in neighborhoods filled with apartment buildings. But single-family neighborhoods can also suffer from loud stereos, barking dogs, and unmuffled car engines. Does the drum corps of the nearby high school practice outside three or four hours a day? Visit the property during periods of high traffic or peak noise. Check noise levels at various times. Even some seemingly tranquil neighborhoods do not offer peace and quiet every hour of the day. Verify.

Ask for Written Disclosures

Seek written disclosures from the seller of the property. Talk with tenants neighbors. Find out whether anyone has tried to enforce quiet by complaining to city government or a homeowners' association or by filing a nuisance suit. If you invest in the property, can you invoke noise ordinances against these noisy tenants (or home owners) who show no respect for anyone else? Can you add features to the property (soundproof windows, heavy doors, more wall insulation, or tall, thickly growing hedges) to abate noise from either outside or inside the building? Suppress noise and you strengthen your MVP.

Overall Desirability: Summing Up

> **To build a great brand, be conscious of the image and the quality of the product. Trump Tower was focused not only on location, but the quality of the building—the windows, floors, rooms, kitchens, the whole thing.**

To create an MVP, provide people a home. As you survey a property, imagine whether the units will live well for your target market:

- Do the units offer enough square footage?
- Are the units spotlessly clean, fresh, and bright? Do they smell clean and fresh?
- Do the room counts and room sizes represent the most profitable use of space?
- Do the aesthetics of the units excite with emotional appeal?
- Does the unit bring in enough natural light?
- What views will the tenants see from inside the units looking out?
- Do the units offer generous amounts of closet and storage space?
- Are the units quiet?
- Will tenants feel safe and secure within the units?
- Do the kitchens and baths offer eye-pleasing pizzazz?

Experience proves that *homes* rent faster and yield lower vacancies than mere rental houses and rental apartments. *Homes* sell faster and command higher prices than mere houses. Offer your tenants and buyers something special. They will pay you higher rents, stay longer, and show more care for their units—because they will regard those units as their home.

10

MORE IDEAS TO CREATE AN MVP

Mr. Trump advises you to evaluate your properties to find multiple uses, multiple streams of income, or even multiple target markets. In the past, developers would construct an office building, a hotel, a condominium project, or perhaps a golf course. One idea, one use, one target market.

For Trump Tower, Mr. Trump thought more creatively. He saw this project as a prime location for upscale retailers who are willing to pay rents of $500 per square foot per year (or more). The high floors of the buildings, he knew, would appeal to the very rich who would value the 5th Avenue address and the expansive views of Central Park, the Hudson River, and New York City itself. As to the problematic middle floors, Mr. Trump envisioned offices but realized he would have to innovatively market them to command the rent levels he wanted.

On all points, his ideas succeeded. As George Ross has observed, "In the late 1970s, Trump's vision of a three-tiered, multiuse condominium represented a very unusual combination of uses." Today, many other builders have tried to imitate this example.

Similarly, when they developed a renovation and leasing plan for the Trump Building (40 Wall Street), George Ross and Mr. Trump decided to pursue a multiuse approach. As George Ross told Mr. Trump, "The experts have been taking the wrong approach and they've reached the wrong conclusion. You don't have one office building, you have three. They just happen to be on top of each other."

So, that's how they renovated and marketed it—to three different market segments. They turned this 1929 building with its outdated configuration and floor plans into a marvelous modern masterpiece with each part of the tower designed to appeal to specific types of tenants. In contrast to its near-vacant status at the time of purchase, this property today stands nearly 100% occupied.

> **Attend to the details. Just like my father, I walk every project. It's my responsibility to make everything look exquisite.**

Y OU'RE ON THE WAY TO creating an MVP (most valued property). You've designed great livable homes that sparkle with pizzazz and emotional appeal. These features will keep your building full of tenants who willingly pay premium prices. Yet before sharp livable interiors can woo your prospective tenants and buyers, you must get them to keep their appointments to inspect the homes that you offer. To accomplish this goal, enhance curb appeal.

To further add even more to your cash flows and property values, provide more services to your tenants, create more rentable space, and revitalize the neighborhood. Any or all of these techniques will create value for tenants, buyers, and you—the very definition of MVP.

CREATE STRIKINGLY ATTRACTIVE CURB APPEAL

You can write an award-winning ad that will make your phone ring. But your Madison Avenue talents will fall flat when great tenants pull up in front of the building and immediately begin to ask themselves, "What are we doing here? This place is nothing like I imagined. Do you think we should go in?"

> **When prospects pull up to your property, make sure they immediately feel, "This looks like a nice place to live."**

"Nah, why waste our time? This place is a dump. We shouldn't even think about living here."

Your Building Is Your Best Advertisement

Hundreds (maybe thousands) of people will pass by your property each week. What will they notice? Will the property become known as that run-down rental of the neighborhood? Or will it cause passersby to remark, "Isn't that building kept up well? Those flower gardens and brick walkways seem to reach out and invite us to take a look inside."

I'm always trying to figure out, "What can I do with this property to give it flair, pizzazz—something my customers can find nowhere else?"

To generate more rental income, create an inviting exterior. Create award-winning publicity with knockout curb appeal. Not only will an attractive, well-kept exterior appeal to a better class of tenants, but it will also increase tenant satisfaction and reduce turnover. To create these strikingly attractive curb appeal, try these improvements:

1. *Clean Up the Grounds:* When you first take over a property, get busy with a meticulous cleanup of the grounds, parking area, and walkways. Pick up trash, accumulated leaves, and fallen tree branches. Build a fence to block that view of the dumpsters. Tell tenants to remove their inoperable cars from the parking lots, parking spaces, or driveways. If abandoned cars are parked on the street, ask the city government to post them and tow them.

2. *Yard Care and Landscaping:* Tenants and home buyers alike love a manicured lawn, flower-lined walkways, mulched shrubs, and flower gardens. With landscaping, you can turn an ugly-duckling building into a showcase property. With landscaping, you can create privacy, manufacture a pleasant view looking out from the inside of the units, or eliminate an ugly sight. Plant trees, shrubs, flower gardens, and hedges now. When you sell, those mature plantings will easily earn you a return of $10 for each $1 the plantings cost you.

3. *Walkways and Parking Areas:* Replace or repair major cracks and buckling that may appear in your sidewalks and parking areas. Remove all grass or weeds that are growing through the cracks. Edge all the areas where the yard

abuts concrete or asphalt. Neatness pays. Overgrown grass and weeds stain the curb appeal of a property—precisely because these types of blemishes often signal that the property is a rental.

4. *Fences, Lampposts, and Mailboxes:* For good looks, privacy, and security, install quality fencing. In contrast, a rusted, rotted, or half-falling-down fence scars the property. Likewise for rusty lampposts with broken glass fixtures. For a decorative touch, add a white picket fence or a low-level stone fence in the front of the building. If the building houses a cluster of mailboxes, keep the area clear of misdelivered letters, junk mail, and discarded advertising circulars.

5. *The Exterior of the Building:* The building should signal to prospective tenants that you take good care of your property. Paint where necessary or desirable. Repair wood rot. Clean roof and gutters.

Imagine ways to enhance the building's appearance with shutters, flower boxes, a dramatic front door and entryway, and new (or additional) windows. Add contrasting colors for trim or accent the building design with architectural details. How well does (or could) the property's exterior distinguish it from other comparably priced rental properties?

Think outside the lines of conventional thought. Move out of your comfort zone and achieve something unique.

Here's How to Dazzle with Curb Appeal

Unless you're creatively gifted, you might not spontaneously generate *great* ideas for improving a property. I know. Creative design doesn't come easily to me. I rank high among the artistically challenged. Here's how to compensate for this dull artistic vision.

Carry a camera in the glove box of your car. When you see a building or yard that displays eye-catching features, snap a picture. Over time, put together a collection of photos. When you try to figure out how to give a property strikingly attractive curb appeal, pull out some of these photos and select model properties to compare feature to feature with your investment property. Compare and contrast to bring forth a rush of value-creating, MVP ideas.

Don't rely exclusively on your own snapshots. Dozens of *Better Homes and Gardens* types of books and magazines fill the shelves of groceries and bookstores. Regularly buy these publications. Their articles and photos will definitely extend your creative thinking and aesthetic sensibilities.

Collect More Than Rent

When you review a property seller's revenue statements, you may see an entry called "other income." These amounts may include revenues received from laundry machines, parking fees, storage lockers, or other services and amenities. Savvy entrepreneurs think of ways to generate extra income from their properties:

1. *Laundry:* Rental units should include washer/dryer hookups. But if they don't, look for space somewhere else on the property where you can install coin-operated (actually electronic card-operated) washers and dryers. Without on-premises laundry facilities, your building will suffer a serious competitive disadvantage. Most good tenants were raised in homes with washer and dryers. These tenants do not want to cart their washings to a distant laundry.
2. *Parking Fees:* If parking spots are scarce in the neighborhood where you own properties, charge extra for parking (or perhaps a fee for a second car). Do not arbitrarily give

one parking space per unit. Some tenants may not have cars. Others may be willing to park on the street. When you price your scarce parking separately from the units, those tenants who want it most will pay more.

3. *Build Storage Lockers:* Back to the idea of adding storage space. You create value anytime you squeeze some profitable use out of every nook and cranny within the building and within every square foot of the site. One such profitable use is storage lockers. Does the property include an attic, basement, or crawl space where you could carve out room for more storage? You can rent lockers for $10 to $20 per month (maybe substantially more, depending on size). Achieve payback in four years or less. If no existing space within the building can serve this purpose, install several of those prefabricated storage buildings.

4. *Add Other Amenities or Services:* Whenever you take over a property, think through a list of services or amenities that you could provide (preferably at a price) that would increase your revenue *and* strengthen your competitive edge for your target market. Consider services such as cleaning, day care, or transportation. As amenities, would your target market appreciate (and pay for) a swimming pool, tennis courts, racquetball or squash courts, a fitness center, or a study room? As investor Craig Hall advises, "Keep an open and searching mind. Seek out things you can do to attract and satisfy the best tenants for each specific investment."

CONVERT A GARAGE, ATTIC, OR BASEMENT TO LIVING SPACE

Look for properties with an attic, garage, or basement that you can convert to *quality* living space. Note the emphasis on *quality*. Amateurs often convert as cheaply as possible. Not only do their finished spaces look cheap, but they may lack natural light, the ceilings may hang too low, or the newly created traffic patterns or floor plans may seem convoluted or garbled. Add quality space, not space that looks weird.

Savvy investors who design and finish their conversions to wow potential tenants or buyers can and do make serious money for their efforts. To contribute to MVP, your conversion should achieve the following objectives:

- Meet the needs of target market.
- Be aesthetically pleasing.
- Be well integrated within the overall plan and design of the property.

Target Market Needs

When you remodel only for personal use, it's okay to convert your basement into a rec room that mimics the look of your favorite tavern. For MVP remodeling, aim to please your target market. What type of highly valued space can you offer that competing properties lack: a dynamite home office, a study, a playroom for the kids, a workout area, a library, an entertainment center, or a seductive master bedroom and bath? Think visually. What can you imagine? Research, "What uses would tenants gladly pay for?"

Aesthetics

Basement conversions often fail because they lack windows and give off that damp, musty odor so common to belowground living areas. To overcome these problems, use window wells and carve outs to bring in natural light. To eliminate the musty smell and dampness, use high-quality sealants and fresh air ventilation. Follow the same general ideas for attic and garage conversions. To command a premium price, these finished areas must look, live, feel, and smell as good as the rest of the house. They must exude light, height, warmth, and color. Do not tack up cheap four- by eight-foot paneling, hang acoustical tile ceilings, or lay down a roll of indoor-outdoor carpeting. Romance the home. Think pizzazz!

Integrate the Conversion into the Units

When you evaluate properties, think how you can integrate any extra living space into a coherent floor plan. MVP conversions flow smoothly to and from the original living areas. Think access and flow. Blend the conversion into a natural traffic pattern.

MVP conversions do not announce themselves as conversions. Avoid signaling to your prospects, "Now entering a converted garage (basement or attic)." Or "Watch your head. The ceiling's a little low in here." A well-planned conversion can pay back $4 (or more) for every dollar you invest.

CREATE AN ACCESSORY APARTMENT

Variously called in-law suites, basement suites, garage apartments, mortgage helpers, or accessory apartments, these separate living units pay back their cost many times over. Depending on the city and neighborhood, an accessory apartment can bring in rents that range anywhere from $250 to $750 per month. And, unless you build from scratch, you can usually create a desirable unit for as little as $5,000 and certainly no more than $15,000 or $20,000.

In terms of return on investment, $10,000 in renovation costs, for example, can generate a rental income of $4,000 to $6,000 per year. You can search the world over and not find as much return for so little risk.

CREATE A SPECIAL PURPOSE USE

You may find that renovating toward some special purpose use might secure you a premium price or rental rate. Most investors go generic. In return, they receive a generic profit. But when you reno-vate toward the specific needs of a bull's-eye segment of seniors, the disabled, children, home businesses, college students, or any other specialized target of tenants (buyers), you favorably distin-guish your product.

To discover a profitable niche, talk with people at social service agencies, hospitals, and local colleges. Imagine the special needs of single parents, multigenerational households, hobbyists, room-mates, group homes, and shelters. Always stay alert for improve-ments where demand runs strong and supply falls short. Whereas most run-of-the-mill investors know how to fix up a property, entre-preneurs search for a special niche of customers. Then they tailor the features of the property to match that target market's MVP.

Change the Use of a Property

Rental apartments now sold as condominiums, gas stations now operating as retail outlets (convenience stores), old homes con-verted to office space, what was once farm acreage now a sprawl-ing urban shopping center—such properties provide examples of adaptive use of both land and buildings brought about by a locale's growth and change.

Adaptive reuse offers multiple opportunities for the entrepre-neur. Office space sometimes rents at twice the rental rate of hous-ing. The opposite also can occur. In London, housing prices have climbed so high that retail, warehouse, and offices are being con-verted to apartments. To create your MVP, adapt the property to a more profitable use.

Convert Apartments to Condominiums

To plan for a condo conversion, study the local area to learn what prices various types of condo units are selling for. Then com-pare those respective condo unit prices to the price per unit that apartment buildings are generating. If you notice a gap in prices of $25,000 or more (sometimes less), you've probably discovered an opportunity to earn profits with an MVP conversion.

Here's how to calculate the potential profits of converting rental units into individually owned condominiums for a 16-unit apartment building:

Acquisition price ($30,000 per unit)	$480,000
Upgrade at $7,500 per unit	$120,000
Attorney fees (condo document preparation, government permitting process, sales contract preparation, closing document review)	$40,000
Marketing costs (advertising, sales commissions)	$45,000
Mortgage interest (12-month renovation and sellout)	$50,000
Incidentals (architect, interior design, landscaping, government permits)	$35,000
Total costs	$770,000
Cost per unit	$48,125

In this example, you paid $480,000 ($30,000 per unit) to acquire this 16-unit rental property. After all costs of conversion, your total investment increased to $770,000 ($48,125 per unit). But these figures haven't yet considered profits. If you want to net $10,000 per unit, you will need to sell the units at a price approaching $60,000 each ($30,000 more than your original per-unit purchase price).

To decide whether such a project makes sense, research rental properties, condo prices, and conversion laws. Run through some feasibility calculations. If preliminary estimates look promising, talk with an investor, contractor, attorney, or real estate consultant experienced in the conversion process. With the knowledge gained from these talks (and perhaps some follow-up research), you can decide whether this investment approach offers you enough profit potential to compensate for such risks as cost overruns, slow sales, and permitting government delays.

The condo conversion business runs in cycles. In the late 1990s, few conversions looked profitable. As condo prices jumped during the early to mid-2000s, conversions multiplied like mushrooms after an April rain. Today, many condo markets seem oversupplied with new construction and conversions. Opportunities for condo conversions have become tougher to find in popular cities.

But the cycle will turn again. Remain alert to profit when new markets evolve. Or look to cities that aren't yet on the mobile investor's radar screen.

CONVERT APARTMENTS OR HOUSES TO OFFICE SPACE

Sometimes it's profitable to convert apartments or houses to office space. To mull over this possibility, answer these questions:

1. Is the property in a commercial zone? If not, can you get the property rezoned?
2. What is the current vacancy rate for office space in the area of the subject property? Are any market segments undersupplied?
3. Do you have adequate parking for office space? The city may require one parking space for every 250 to 500 square feet of rentable office space.
4. How much will it cost to convert? Could you borrow the money to finance such a conversion? And, finally, will the cost, legal procedures, and time and effort be worth the eventual profit you will realize?

Study the property, current and future demand, and supply. Figure the costs and rental revenues of the projected conversion. For more complex projects, partner with someone who is more experienced.

Place the promising property under an option or purchase contract with contingencies. Then line up your partner and proceed.

Cut Operating Expenses

As a rule of thumb, every dollar you slice from your property's operating expenses can add $10 or more to your building's value. With gains like that, meticulously keep track of all expenses. Then make continuous efforts to reduce, shift, or eliminate them. Lower operating costs not only increase your net cash flows but also permit you to offer tenants more attractive rents. Here are some ideas to cut expenses.

Energy Audits

Utility companies will help you discover ways to reduce your gas and/or electric bills. Some will even audit and inspect your property. Others will provide booklets or brochures and, perhaps, a customer service department to answer specialized questions. You can also find dozens of articles and books at your local library that discuss energy conservation. Perform an energy audit on a building before you buy it. Then you can judge beforehand the extent to which you can feasibly reduce these costs.

Maintenance and Repair Costs

Savvy investors reduce or eliminate money-wasting property maintenance and repair expenses. Focus on the following:

1. *Low-Maintenance Houses and Apartment Buildings:* When shopping to buy, favor those properties that are constructed with materials; heating, ventilating, and air-conditioning; and fixtures that require less maintenance. Nothing beats a property that's built to last with minimal care. Ditto for yards, shrubs, and landscaping.

2. *Tenant Selection:* Just as there are both low- and high-maintenance properties, so too are there low- and high-maintenance tenants. Avoid the latter and select the former. Watch out for chronic complainers and people who show no "house sense."

3. *Repair Clauses:* To promote tenant responsibility, a growing number of property owners shift the first $50 or $100 of every repair cost onto their tenants' shoulders. Also, I favor high security deposits.

4. *Handyman on Call:* Nothing eases the drain on your time and pocketbook as much as having a trustworthy and competent all-around handyman (or persons) to take care of your property maintenance and repairs.

5. *Preventive Maintenance:* You periodically inspect and maintain your car. Do likewise with your investment properties. Anticipate and alleviate when the cost is relatively small. Always ask your maintenance experts how to substitute high-maintenance items or materials with low-maintenance replacements.

Property Taxes

"If you think that your property taxes are too high," writes tax consultant Harry Koenig, "you're probably right! Research shows that nearly half of all properties may be assessed illegally or excessively." While Koenig probably overstates his point, millions of property owners do pay more in property taxes than they need to. With a little attention and planning, you can avoid this trap:

1. *Check the Accuracy of Your Assessed Valuation:* Usually, tax assessors base their tax calculations on a property's market value. Look closely at the assessor's value estimate on your tax bill. Can you find comparable sales of similar properties that would support a *lower* value for your property? If so, you have grounds to request a tax reduction.

2. *Compare Your Purchase Price to the Assessor's Estimate of Market Value:* Provide comp sales. Show the assessor that you recently paid $190,000 for a property that he has appraised at $240,000. You've got a prima facie case for lower taxes.

3. *Look for Unequal Treatment:* Under the law, assessors must tax properties in a neighborhood in an equal (fair) and uniform manner. You can argue for lower taxes by showing that the assessor has assigned lower values to similar nearby properties.

4. *Learn Tax Assessment Laws before You Improve or Rehabilitate a Property:* The property tax laws of every state list the types of property improvements that are taxed and the applicable rates. After you discover the fine print of such laws, develop your property improvement strategy to add value without adding taxes.

GENTRIFICATION AND OTHER VALUE PLAYS

In large- and medium-sized cities across the United States and Canada, gentrification has pushed property prices through the roof in neighborhoods like Kerrisdale (Vancouver), Buckhead (Atlanta), South of Market (San Francisco), Chicago North Side, Chicago West Side, College Park (Orlando), "M Street" (Dallas), and Coconut Grove (Miami). Most of these neighborhoods have become name brands.

In earlier years, though, most of these neighborhoods were modest, even lower-priced neighborhoods. Several areas, such as Chicago Near North, San Francisco South of Market, and Manhattan's Soho districts, included industrial and commercial properties.

In each instance, however, the close-in accessibility of these neighborhoods overwhelmed their negatives. Even prior to gaining cachet, these neighborhoods gave residents an easy walk, drive, or commute to major job districts. And their prices looked dirt cheap when compared with conveniently situated premier neighborhoods.

Many gentrified name-brand neighborhoods no longer represent good value. That's not to say that these areas won't show strong future appreciation. But, as a rule, their current rent levels probably won't cover a reasonable-sized mortgage payment plus property expenses.

**Play up your location. Point out every advantage.
Turn every negative into a positive.**

The Good News

But here's the good news. All across the country, other emerging neighborhoods are poised for turnaround, revitalization, and rapid appreciation of property values. By becoming a neighborhood entrepreneur, you can score the same large gains that those early investors have earned in College Park, Near North, and Thorton Park.

Revitalize the Neighborhood

You've heard it a 100 times: "Buy in the best neighborhood you can afford. The best neighborhoods appreciate the most. You can change anything about a property except its location." At first glance, this advice seems plausible. But think what the term *neighborhood* actually refers to:

- Convenience.
- Aesthetics.
- People: attitudes, lifestyles.
- Legal restrictions.
- Schools.
- Taxes/services.
- Microclimate (weather).
- Safety and security.
- Image/reputation.
- Affordability.

In an article on home buying, *Money* magazine advised its readers, "It's a great time to shop for your dream house. . . . You'll need to seek out the neighborhoods where property values are rising faster than your community average." Surprising to many investors, though, the neighborhoods where prices will rise fastest may not be the name-brand or well-established neighborhoods. Often, the largest price increases will occur in areas that are positioned and poised for turnaround or renewed popularity. The "best" neighborhoods don't always appreciate the fastest.

Entrepreneurs Improve Thorton Park (and Make a Killing)

"Florida's new urban entrepreneurs have the vision to see a bustling district of sushi bars, loft apartments and boutiques on a glass-strewn lot or rat-infested warehouse," writes Cynthia Barnett in an issue of *Florida Trend* magazine.

Phil Rampy is proud to have been one of those early entrepreneurs. Twelve years ago, Rampy bought a property in the then-shunned Thorton Park neighborhood near trash-strewn Lake Eola (or, as they used to call is, Lake Erie-ola). Today, Thorton Park has climbed up the status ladder to rank among "the trendiest addresses" in Orlando. That $60,000 bungalow that Rampy renovated is now valued at more than $200,000. Although Thorton Park still sits on this Earth in the same place as it did 10 years ago, nearly everything else about this neighborhood has changed.

Many Neighborhoods Have Potential

When you compare neighborhoods, look at the present but imagine the future. Learn what people are saying about different neighborhoods. List all of a neighborhood's good points. How could you and other property owners join together to highlight and improve these features? List the neighborhood's weak points. How can you and others eliminate negative influences? Who can you enlist to promote your cause? Can you mobilize mortgage lenders, other

investors, home owners, real estate agents, not-for-profit housing groups, church leaders, builders, contractors, preservationists,
police, local employers, retail businesses, schoolteachers, principals,
community redevelopment agencies, elected officials, civic groups,
and perhaps students, professors, and administrators of a nearby
college or university? People can make a difference.

How to Become a Neighborhood Entrepreneur

You don't have to live in a big-trouble, inner-city location to become
an urban entrepreneur. You can do it anywhere. No neighborhood
is perfect. I suspect that even Beverly Hills and Scarsdale could
stand an improvement or two.

**You can improve any location. Do something radical.
Lead people to think about it in a new way.**

Since neighborhood quality drives up property values and rent
levels, stay alert for ideas to initiate (or join in) to make the neighborhood a better place to live. When you simultaneously improve
your property(ies) *and* its neighborhood, you more than double
your profit potential. Would any of the following suggestions work
for the areas that you can discover?

Add to Neighborhood Convenience

Would a stoplight, wider road, or new highway interchange improve
accessibility to the neighborhood? Where are the to-and-fro traffic
logjams? How can they be alleviated? Is the neighborhood served
as well as it could be by buses and commuter trains? How about
social service transportation? Could you get the vans that pick
up seniors or the disabled to include this neighborhood on their
route? What about the traveling bus for the library? Does it stop
in the neighborhood? Try to attract new retailers, coffeehouses,
and restaurants.

Improve Appearances and Aesthetics

Fix-up becomes contagious. Put together a civic pride organization. Organize a cleanup and fix-up campaign. Plant trees, shrubs, and flowers in yards and in public areas. Lobby the city to tear down or eliminate eyesore buildings, graffiti, or trashy areas. Reduce on-street parking. Get junk vehicles towed. Enforce environmental regulations against property owners and businesses that pollute (noise, smoke, odors).

Zoning and Building Regulations

Are property owners in the neighborhood splitting up single-family houses and converting them into apartments? Do residents run businesses out of their homes and garages? Are high- or mid-rise buildings planned that will diminish livability? Are commercial properties encroaching on the area? Then lobby for tighter zoning and building regulations. Or do areas within the neighborhood and those nearby make commercial and high-density uses desirable? Then lobby the city to rezone the area to apartments, office, or retail.

Eliminate Neighborhood Nuisances

Do one or more households in the neighborhood make a nuisance of themselves? Junk cars in the driveway, barking dogs, loud stereos, constant yelling and shouting, yards littered with trash—you and other property owners can force them to conform to more acceptable standards of behavior and property upkeep.

Pore over your local ordinances and any applicable homeowners' association rules and restrictions. Sort through regulations on zoning, aesthetics, noise, occupancy, use, parking, disturbing the peace, health, safety, loitering, drug dealing or possession, and assault. You will find some regulatory code that you can cite to uphold a complaint. Rules seldom permit nuisances to continue if complaints are registered.

If after receiving an order to desist neighbors continue to offend common decency, a judge can issue an order. Further violations could then penalize the riffraff for contempt of court. They've now angered the judge. Each day the breach persists could rack up multiple fines and possibly jail time. In some cases, the government will directly remedy the problem—cut the weeds, haul off a junk car—and then bill the offenders.

Upgrade the Schools

The Wall Street Journal reports that all across the country, "parents and property owners are aggressively pushing to improve their public schools." When you think that in many areas parents spend $5,000 to $25,000 a year to send their kids to private schools, it makes economic sense to reallocate those monies into the neighborhood schools. Improve school performance, and your property rents and values will set new highs.

Safety and Security

Enhance safety within the neighborhood (especially for children and seniors) by slowing down or rerouting traffic. Get the city to lay down speed bumps, and you achieve both objectives at the same time. Speed bumps force motorists to let up on the gas pedal, and they direct drivers who want to speed to alternative streets.

Also lobby for lower posted speed limits and intense enforcement. In Berkeley, California, neighborhoods persuaded the city to build concrete traffic blocks at select residential intersections. These road barriers transformed through streets into cul-de-sacs.

Lobby the City Government

You will pay property taxes. Insist that you get the city services that taxes support. The Berkeley experience shows that when neighborhood property owners and residents join together to form a force, they can push the city politicos to alleviate traffic problems, clean the streets, enforce ordinances, upgrade the schools, beef up police patrols, create parks, and provide other services that neighborhoods should expect.

Add Luster to the Neighborhood's Image

Friends of mine used to live in Miami, Florida, but now they live in the upscale village of Pinecrest, Florida. Did they move? No. They and their neighbors persuaded the U.S. Postal Service to give them a new address that would distinguish them from that diverse agglomeration known as Miami. As part of their efforts to create an improved neighborhood, some residents of Sepulveda have formed a new community and renamed it North Hill. In Maryland, Gaithersburg changed its name to North Potomac, attempting to capitalize on the prestige of its nearby neighbor. Residents of North Hollywood got the official name for part of their community changed to Valley Village. "With the name change," says real estate agent Jerry Burns, "residents take more pride in their neighborhood." To improve perception, give your neighborhood or community a new name.

Most properties have hidden potential. It's your job to find it.

Talk Up the Neighborhood

Most people learn about various neighborhoods through word of mouth and articles they read in their local newspapers. As all good publicists know, you can positively influence these efforts to "get the word out." Talk up the neighborhood to opinion leaders. Comment to friends, coworkers, relatives, and acquaintances abut the great improvements of the community. Convince a reporter to play up the neighborhood's potential for turnaround, quality of life, convenience, or affordability. Let everyone know that the area deserves a better image—that the old reputation is no longer accurate. When you revitalize a neighborhood, your properties can double or triple in value within just 5 or 10 years.

11

MARKET YOUR PROPERTY FOR TOP DOLLAR

> **I create the best properties in the world. But I make sure my customers know about it. Because my properties deserve promotion, the press regards me as a master of publicity and marketing.**

Y OU'VE GIVEN your property curb appeal. You've renovated the interior to meet every want, need, and expectation of your potential tenants (buyers). You've revitalized the neighborhood. You know that your target market will reward you with their MVP (most valued property) award. So what's left to do?

Since you've built a better mousetrap, won't the world now beat a path to your door? Maybe, but don't count on it. Properties rarely sell or rent themselves for top dollar.

To earn the highest profits, to reach and persuade your prospects, plan your promotion and advertising (the Transfer process) just as you have planned your property improvements. (Transfer process is *T* in DUST)

WHOM DO YOU WANT TO REACH?

In crafting renovations, think how to create a select type of buyers or tenants. Learn all you can about these prospects. Who are they? Where do they work? Where do they shop? What publications do they read? What clubs, organizations, and trade or professional associations do they belong to? What churches do they attend? In what colleges are they enrolled? Who are their friends, coworkers, or relatives who currently live in the area? What social service agencies cater to their needs? Precisely, what do their demographics and psychographics look like?

Why So Many Questions?

Answer these and similar questions. Otherwise, you will waste time, money, and effort with ill-worded, ill-designed, and misdirected promotions and sales messages. You want to rent or sell this property as quickly as possible. To achieve this result with the least amount of time, effort, and expense, work smarter. The more you know about your potential customers, the better you can figure out what to say and where to spread the word about your property. Why spend big bucks for unproductive advertising in a major newspaper if a well-written notice on a bulletin board will immediately make your telephone ring? Publicize, advertise, and promote your property in those places where you can reach your target market most cost effectively.

Sell Benefits, Not Just the Property

As you think about who you're trying to reach, remember the marketing maxim, "People don't buy features, they buy benefits." Yet many property owners fail to craft a persuasive promotional message. They take five minutes to jot down the usual features of their property. They phone in the ad to a newspaper. What results is nothing more than a generic, unexciting property description such as the following:

> Park Terrace: Split plan, 3-br, 2-bth, den, 2-car garage, 1650 sq. ft., large lot, close to schools and shopping. For more information, call (555)123–4567 after 5:00 p.m.

Standing by itself, this ad may seem okay. But standing in the classified section of a newspaper surrounded by dozens or maybe hundreds of other ads, it does little to grab the target prospect's attention and shout, "Here's the home you've been looking for. Here's why you will want to rush over to see this property right now."

Draw your market segment into the ad. Motivate them to call. Emphasize benefits. Don't trust their imagination. Don't mistakenly believe that if prospects need more information, they will call. You compete with too many other properties for that slapdash approach to perform well. Prospects seldom call just to get more information. They call when out of all the ads they looked through, your ad excited them enough to make the final cut.

Pros tell advertisers, "Sell the sizzle, not just the steak." Describe a property's features in ways that push your prospect's hot buttons. Sergeant Friday of *Dragnet* may be pleased with a "Just the facts, Ma'am" approach. But you need to sell the sizzle.

Sell the Sizzle

So that returns us to these questions:

1. Who are your prospects?
2. What benefits do you offer that distinguish your property from competing properties?

Are your prospects looking for one or more of these benefits?

- Bright with natural light.
- Spacious open floor plan, wonderful for entertaining.
- Quiet street.
- Home warranty, no repair costs for at least two years.
- Top-rated school district.
- Unlimited storage space.
- Bargain price (rent).
- Mortgage helper in-suite.
- Warranted new roof.
- Great appreciation potential.
- Low cost of upkeep.
- Choose your own cabinets, carpets, and colors.
- Owner will carry financing.
- Safe and secure neighborhood.
- Prestigious address/community.
- Energy-saving, low utility bills.
- Lowest price (rent) in neighborhood.
- Low down payment.
- Seller pays closing costs.
- Walk to shops, cafés, library, and restaurants.

- Easy qualifying assumable financing.
- Drop-dead-gorgeous kitchens and bathrooms.
- Private setting.
- Serene views.
- Immaculate condition, pride of ownership.
- Short-term lease/furnished.
- Instant Internet with high-speed cable.
- Utilities paid.
- Clean and fresh.
- Well-insulated, low utility bills.

Inventory your property and its competitors. Note every feature and matching benefit that will excite your tenants (buyers). Which of these features and benefits will best motivate your prospects to call? Which of these features and benefits do most of your competitors fail to provide? If you've strategically crafted your MVP, you can now strategically craft a sales message that will get your property rented (or sold).

CRAFTING A NEWSPAPER AD

In a false economy, many owners cut their classified ads too short. They list a few cold property facts and then expect prospects to call for more information. Don't waste time and money with such meager efforts. Especially when selling a property, if you choose to advertise, include the following information:

- Sizzling hot buttons.
- Square footage.
- Room count.
- Street address.
- Rent (price).
- Terms, if any.
- Amenities.

- Open-house hours.
- Lot size/landscaping.
- Telephone number/Web site.

As an FRBO (for rent by owner) or FSBO (for sale by owner), avoid the tactics that property management and sales agencies follow. Contrary to what most people believe, real estate sales and management firms usually do not run ads to rent or sell specific houses. They run ads to generate prospects for agents. Then, once the agent hooks the prospect, they set off to tour a number of properties. Eventually, the agent hopes to find some property the prospect wants, but agents don't particularly care which property (except they do prefer to push their own listings).

You can't play this numbers game. If you do not hit your targeted buyers with the information they're looking for, your ad won't get circled. Or a misdirected or sparsely worded ad may generate lots of calls from tire kickers, looky-loos, and people who want something other than what you're offering. Poor advertising (especially when linked with overpricing) goes a long way to explain why some owners fail to sell or rent their FSBO/FRBO properties and end up listing with a real estate firm (which costs them even more time and money). The better you tell, the more you sell.

Rather than merely ask people to call for more information, spark their enthusiasm to call with feature/benefit enticements. This ad suggests how to draft an effective sales message:

Affordable—Spacious—Stunning

Mint condition. 3/2, 1840 s. ft. $6,000 d.p., $830 per mo., romantic 400 sq. ft. Master BR suite with fplc., open living area, flower garden views, light and bright kitchen delight, unlimited storage. $160,000— compare at $175,000! 210 Pecan. Open Sat. & Sun. 12–5. Rare find, please call 555-555-1234.

Notice how this ad blends facts and benefits. It conveys a comparative advantage (a value proposition that beats competitors).

It emphasizes the need to "jump on this one" before it's gone. This approach follows the well-known format of AIDA:

- Attention (headlined benefits).
- Interest (condition and affordability).
- Desire (prized features and benefits).
- Action (open house, rare bargain, please call).

This ad will make the phone ring with motivated prospects. If you deliver as promised, you'll sell the first weekend. To lease rather than sell, incorporate the same AIDA principles. Just state rent in lieu of price but still favorably compare your property in significant ways to competing properties.

The Line Count Game

In most cities, newspaper classified ads don't come cheap. As you craft your ad, look for ways to sell the sizzle—but do so with no more words than necessary. It's a good idea to write your ad, let it sit for a day or two, then revise for power and brevity. In the previously suggested ad, depending on line breaks, I may have dropped "rare find, please call."

By using "rare find," I wanted to emphasize scarcity—but most likely my prospects would know that without my telling them. With "please call," I wanted to convey "friendly, courteous" owner. Necessary? Worth another line charge? You be the judge.

To play the line count game, you also must address the issue of abbreviations. How many abbreviations are too many? Are the abbreviated terms easily understood by your prospects? To a degree, newspaper policy controls the answer to these questions because many papers prohibit and limit some abbreviated terms. If permissible, verify clarity and realize that heavy use of abbreviations cheapens your property. Aim to draft cost-effective ads, not ads with the lowest cost.

Depend More on Flyers and Promotional Brochures

Advertising costs money—sometimes quite a lot. For less than the price of a three-day, four-line ad, you can print 500 (or more) promotional flyers. Plus, a flyer gives you much more space for your message and creativity. It also permits you to more closely target your market segment of prospects. As with advertising, give your flyer's sales message some sizzle. Avoid the bland random lists of features as are shown in Figure 11.1. This actual flyer illustrates how not to write a sales message.

Brochures and flyers provide an effective, low-cost way to inform, persuade, and motivate your prospects.

By-Owner Flyer

You can easily see that this by-owner sales sheet (Figure 11.1) fails to provide persuasive copy. But here are several more suggestions:

1. *Never Let "For Sale by Owner" Dominate:* Use an attention-grabbing headline that conveys a strong benefit to the targeted prospects.
2. *Place One or More Photos of the Property on the Flyer:* Photos help jog the prospect's memory and, if done well, can accent the sales message. Use a digital camera and print color flyers from your computer. Black-and-white photocopies cheapen you and the property.
3. *Organize Your Information in Related Sections:* Emphasize the strongest features and benefits.
4. *Explain Possibilities:* Notice that this property is zoned commercial. What does that mean for the value and uses of the property? Do not leave property potential to the buyer's imagination. (Of course, as an entrepreneurial investor, you will actively search for properties that offer potential that sellers either do not recognize or undervalue.)

FOR SALE or RENT
BY OWNER

612 NW 3rd Street

4 Bedroom / 2 Bath

approx. **1550 sq. ft.**

Large corner lot with 6ft. wood privacy fence in backyard

Central Heat and A/C (one bedroom has separate wall mount A/C)

Appliances: Washer, Dryer, Refrigerator, Stove

Ceiling fans in each room

Zoned: Office/Residential (currently residential)

FOR SALE
$85,000

FOR RENT
$975 / month

Available 11-15
(First, Last, and $500 Security deposit required)

Call **(123)-456-7890** for more information or to schedule a visit.

Figure 11.1   By-Owner Flyer.

To communicate MVP, list and explain advantages of your property. Otherwise, your sales message can zip right past those people who would value your property most highly. How many sales messages hit you and everyone else every day? At least hundreds, probably thousands. Persuasively motivate your prospects. Cut through the advertising clutter that by necessity everyone must block from consciousness.

Rewrite of the By-Owner Flyer

Read through the rewrite (Figure 11.2) of the by-owner flyer (Figure 11.1). Notice that this rewrite raises the price. Why? Because the owner was trying to sell a run-down property. In contrast, this revised message sells the promise of making money. When the present lacks obvious appeal, sell the future. (As a buyer, pay for the present, get the future for free.)

Also notice that the new flyer is loaded with facts and benefits. The more you tell, the more you sell. Look at any successful immediate response sales message. Whether it's a television infomercial or a magazine ad, advertisers load their direct sales messages with features and benefits. They try to persuade prospects that their proposition offers customers the best value available (an MVP). Emphasize facts and benefits that strongly appeal to your market.

Distribute Flyers to Your Target Market

People drive through neighborhoods to look for "for sale" and "for rent" properties that interest them. So first put the flyers in a waterproof tube or pouch and hang them on the large, easily read for-sale or for-rent sign that you place in the front yard of the property. In addition, distribute copies of the flyer anywhere your targeted prospects can see them:

- Neighborhood bulletin boards (such as those in grocery stores, libraries, and coffeeshops).
- Neighborhood residents.
- People you know at work, church, and clubs.

◊ **Cosmetic Fixer**   ◊ **Bargain Price**
◊ **Loaded with Profit Potential**

612 NW 3ʳᵈ St.– 4/2/1550 sq. ft.

$95,000 –Terms Possible/Lease-Option/Rent

PHOTO	PHOTO	PHOTO

Zoned Office/Residential– Great Income Property

with Rehab/Conversion Upside

Location	*Exterior and Site*	*Interior*
◊ Growing high-traffic corridor	◊ Low-maintenance conrete block	◊ Easy office conversion
◊ 5 minutes or less to downtown,	◊ 4-year-old roof	◊ In-suite possibility
◊ the university, major retail	◊ 1/2-acre lot with up to 12-car	◊ Plaster soundproof walls
◊ 3% office vacancy rate in area	parking	◊ Nearly new energy-efficient
◊ Neighborhood revitalization in	◊ Building expansion possible	Heat/AC
progress		

My Loss, Your Gain:
Owner relocation.
Lowest price per sq. ft. in area.
Will sell, lease, or lease option.
Make offer.

Cosmetic fix-up will net you a high return.

Will show at your convenience

(123) 456-7890
Realtor coop @ 3% $250 Birdog Reward

Figure 11.2   Rewrite of By-Owner Flyer.

- Neighborhood churches.
- Mortgage companies and real estate firms.
- Schools, colleges, and employers.
- Home-buyer counseling agencies.
- Apartment complexes (if you don't get thrown off the property).

Don't wait for buyers to find you. Bring your opportunity to them. At any given moment, many prospects for your property aren't actively searching. They're procrastinating. They're waiting for your sales message to motivate them. Hand out your flyers to anyone and everyone who might know of a potential buyer (or tenant). Unleash your bird dogs. Plug into your network.

I have bought and sold many properties through word of mouth. Unbelievably, few by-owners play this technique for all that its worth.

Make Your Sign Stand Out

Use the largest for-rent or for-sale sign that the law (or homeowners' association rule) allows. Place as much appealing sales information as possible. Just like your flyer and classified ads, your sign must grab *A*ttention, create *I*nterest, generate *D*esire, and motivate passersby to *A*ction (AIDA). Someone driving by at 40 miles per hour should be able to recognize the great deal that you're offering. To read your sign, drivers should not have to stop and get out of their car.

Sell with Honesty

Your sales message should sell the sizzle, but you need to deliver the steak. You're entitled to tout the advantages of your property. No one's entitled to fabricate features that don't exist or that cover up serious negatives that detract from the property. If you misrepresent the property, you lose credibility, waste your own time, and waste the time and efforts of your prospects.

> **Don't con your customers. Bravado, hyperbole, that's the preview to the show. But when the curtain rises, deliver what the audience came to see.**

Strive to give your tenants and buyers the best deal for their money. Do not dupe them into paying too much for too little. Establish a strong reputation, and prospects will come to you and inquire, "When do you think that you'll have something else coming for rent (sale)? Please give us a call." MVP not only stands for "most valued property" but also signals "most valuable player"—that's you.

Don't Merely Show the Property, Sell It

Your promotional efforts have worked their magic. Are you planning to *show* the property? Throw away that idea. Rewind your sales program. Erase the notion that you are going to *show* the property. You are going to *rent* or *sell* it, not merely show it. Selling a property requires a different perspective.

When people show properties, they stand back in a passive role. They let the buyer wander around, and, if asked, they try to answer a question or two. When the prospect begins to leave, the passive showman says, "Thanks for coming by. Let me know if you think you might be interested," or, "Here's a rental application. Would you like to take one with you?"

The persuasive owner knows that prospects arrive full of hopes, fears, and uncertainties. The persuasive owner *prepares* to address all these buyer concerns. "Let me know if you have any questions" does not make a sales presentation.

Sales Success: Your 12-Step Program

To move past showing and on to selling, follow these 12 steps to a successful close (lease or purchase agreement). This 12-step program will convert prospects into renters or buyers.

Back Up Your Sizzle with Facts

Collect data on comps. Photocopy pertinent regulatory ordinances. Provide a home warranty. Show school rankings. Map out the convenience of the location to important linkages (employers, shopping, culture, nightlife, parks, schools). Whatever persuasive points you want to make, secure documentary proof or confirming evidence. Without facts, you're just puffing.

Establish Rapport

Find common ground for chitchat. Before you extol kitchens and closets, find out about their kids, cars, or hobbies. "I see you're wearing an Illini sweatshirt. Is that where you went to college?" "Really, you did? My son graduates from U of I this year."

Segue into Likes and Dislikes

Never talk features and benefits until you've learned the prospects' hot buttons and turnoffs. "What would you like to see first? What features prompted your call? Would you like . . . ?" Too often, owners and real estate agents launch into a monologue about features that prospects care little about. Or, worse, they tout features that prospects find unappealing. This drives buyers into a socially distant position. Out goes your rapport.

Diplomatically Discover Their Feelings about Other Properties They've Shopped

You think that you're offering a great property that will win your prospect's MVP award. But what do your prospects think? Seek feedback about the market from the only people who really count—your potential renters and buyers.

Really Listen to the Criticism That Prospects Give You

You've worked hard to renovate the property to beat the competition. But, hey, none of us is perfect. Maybe you have overlooked something. Ask your prospects for objections and weak points. Until you get a signed contract, keep searching for profit-enhancing improvements.

Translate Features into Easily Understood Benefits

Your prospects won't necessarily see the meaning of R-38 insulation, thermo pane windows, a southern exposure, or R-1B zoning. Translate those features into benefits. "This heavy-grade insulation means that your heat and air costs will run less than $100 a month. Once this zoysia grass matures, your yard will look like a putting green, and you'll never have to pull crabgrass or weeds. Look at this photo. That's how the yard will look by the end of summer."

Inform the Prospective Buyers about Financing

First-time buyers, especially, may know little about down payments, monthly payments, and closing costs. They may not realize that they can buy your property with only a few thousand cash out of pocket (which they may borrow from relatives). They may not realize that their after-tax monthly house payments can cost them less than rent.

If you're selling to investors, work the numbers into your sales presentation. Investors want to learn about rents, cash flows, expenses, vacancy rates, and expected rates of return (see Chapter 14).

Monitor the Prospects' Dialogue, Emotional Responses, and Body Language

Are the prospects mentally moving their furniture into the home? Are they working through the financials in the context of their budget or investment goals? Are they voicing seriously considered objections about rent, deposit, price, terms, features, or neighborhood? Intensity of interest, both positive and negative, signals that they want to rent or buy—if you can alleviate their concerns and strengthen the facts and evidence that support (what you believe to be) an MVP offer.

Make It Easy to Complete a Written Agreement

Prepare your paperwork ahead of time. When you detect or elicit buy signals, move to the kitchen table (or sofa and coffee table) that you've brought into the unit (if it's vacant). When the prospects hesitate to commit, give assurances along with the reasons they need to act now and not let this great MVP go to someone else. If necessary, agree to include short-term contingencies. However, retain the right to accept backup offers. If such an offer does come in, you agree to give the original buyers (tenants) 24 hours (possibly longer) to clear their contingency or else lose their chance to own (lease) the property.

Set Up an Earnest-Money Escrow for Buyers

To seal the deal, buyers will put up an earnest-money deposit. If they're smart, they won't make out this check directly to you. So prearrange an escrow account with a title company (or other escrow agent). The buyers can then write the check directly to the escrow account. This technique gives the buyers more confidence that you're playing straight with them.

Follow Up a Successful Signing

When you successfully sign your buyers or tenants, follow up to achieve two goals: (1) Make sure they proceed quickly to satisfy their contingencies (property inspection, mortgage approval, lawyer consultation) and (2) keep them motivated.

Some prospects suffer buyer's remorse. They begin to doubt their decision. You treat this disease with periodic positive updates: "A property down the street just sold for $10,000 more than you paid. The neighborhood elementary school has won an award for outstanding extracurricular programs. The city has just pledged $500,000 to upgrade neighborhood streets and parks."

After prospects sign an agreement, assure them that they've made the right decision. Do what you can to bolster their high feelings of excitement. Alleviate their low feelings of regret and uncertainty.

Follow Up an Unsuccessful Close

When you set an appointment to rent or sell the property, get the full names of the prospects and their telephone numbers. If you meet prospects through an open house that you're holding, ask visitors to register (name and phone number) for a door-prize drawing. Or when convenient, directly ask for their names and numbers (or business cards).

Find out who your active prospects are and how to keep in touch. Follow up with a thank-you note and more persuasive information about the property. Too many FRBOs and FSBOs let active prospects walk out the door, never to be heard from again. Avoid that mistake. Reignite their interest, desire, and action with periodic updates about the property, the availability of lower-rate financing, or other potentially motivating developments. Even prospects who are "just looking" today may become your tenants or buyers tomorrow.

12

The Eight Steps of Successful Management

**You run your operation well, you make a good profit.
Run it first class, you'll multiply your bank balances.**

You've created the MVP (most valued property) and attracted a quality tenant; you've verified credit, income, and references; and you've signed a lease. Your entrepreneurial strategy will soon begin to pay off. You're missing only one critical piece of the wealth-building puzzle. You need a management system.

In this chapter, you will learn how to maximize your cash flows while minimizing your worry. A good management plan assures your customers that they will receive the benefits they expect. It assures you of wealth without worry. Now, your first question: Should you delegate property management or do it yourself?

**Ferdinand Marcos (and other owners) mismanaged 40
Wall Street into steep disrepair. Their management
destroyed value. My management system created
enormous value for the property because it blends
a great building and location with exemplary tenant
services.**

Self-Manage or Employ a Management Firm

If you are a beginning investor, I encourage you to self-manage your properties. After you build up your portfolio of rentals, withdraw from the day-to-day activities if you choose to. Self-management offers you these advantages:

- You'll save money. You'll eliminate the costs that you would otherwise pay to a management company, and, by self-contracting your own repair work (or by doing it yourself), you will spend less.

- Your vacant units will rent faster. Whenever I see a long-term vacancy, 90 percent of the time that property is being "professionally" managed. Management firms seldom work diligently to fill vacancies. They're content to put up a sign, *maybe* run an ad, and merely wait for a rental prospect to show up. You can do much better than that.

- You'll discover the ins and outs, the good and bad, of property management. Although I do not now handle the day-to-day work of my property operations, the knowledge and experiences I gained from those early do-it-myself years are still paying off. If you've never done it yourself, how will you be able to design (or critique) the management practices, policies, and procedures of your property manager?

- As you talk with prospective renters, look at competing properties, and monitor vacancies and rent levels, you build an invaluable firsthand base of market information. If you listen, that market knowledge will tell you how to choose the most profitable target market of tenants and how to adapt your property, lease terms, and rental rates to establish a competitive advantage.

For beginning investors, the advantages of self-management beat hired guns who do it only for the money. Even Robert Griswald (author of *Property Management for Dummies* and owner of a large property management firm) agrees. Griswald advises,

> If you have the right temperament for managing property, and if you have the time and live in the vicinity of your property(ies), you should definitely do it yourself. (14)

Regardless of whether you or a firm provides management for your property, this eight-step management system (listed next) will help you achieve an MVP status for yourself (most valuable player) and your tenants (most valued property).

The Eight Steps of Successful Property Management

1. Design a lease for your target market.
2. Create a flawless move-in.
3. Retain top-flight residents.
4. When the market supports it, raise rents.
5. Anticipate and prepare for special problems.
6. Maintain the property.
7. Process move-outs smoothly.
8. Persistently find ways to increase your cash flow.

DESIGN A LEASE FOR YOUR TARGET MARKET

By far, most small-property owners treat their lease strictly as a document that they can use to compel tenant performance. Although imperfect in that respect, written leases do give you more legal protection than an oral agreement. But your leases also should serve another important purpose: They should help you achieve a competitive advantage over other property owners.

Your Lease Clauses

Before you decide on the specific clauses within your lease, closely review the leases of other property owners. Look for ways to differentiate your rental agreement that would encourage tenants (your target market) to choose your property over competing properties. For example, you might gain a competitive advantage by lowering your up-front cash requirements, offering a repair guarantee, shortening your lease term, guaranteeing a lease renewal without an increase in rent, or placing tenant security deposits and last month's rent in the investment of the tenant's choice to accrue interest or appreciation for the tenant's benefit.

Or, alternatively, perhaps you could develop very "tight" or "restrictive" lease clauses and position your property as rentals that cater to more discriminating and responsible tenants. You could include severe restrictions on noise and other nuisances common to rentals. In that way, you could promote your property as "the quiet place to live."

In other words, you create competitive advantage not only by adapting the features of your property to the wants of your tenant market but also by custom tailoring the clauses, language, and length of your lease to match tenant needs.

Explain Your Advantages

By adapting leases to better fit the needs of your target market, you can increase your rental revenues, achieve a higher rate of occupancy, and/or lower your operating expenses. To fully realize these benefits, though, make sure that prospective tenants recognize and understand the advantages you're offering. Adopt the strategy of a successful salesman. Rather than show your property, point out and explain (from the tenants' standpoint) the desirable features of both the unit and your lease.

In crafting a lease to fit your market strategy, dozens of items, issues, and contingencies present themselves for possible inclusion. Although "typical" practices are featured in the following discussions, stay alert for ways to creatively adapt (or omit) items to better appeal to your tenants. Properly drafted, your lease can materially boost your efforts to attract premium tenants. In contrast, archaic legal jargon and an authoritarian demeanor can drive good tenants into the rentals offered by your competitors.

CREATE A FLAWLESS MOVE-IN

Confirm the cleanliness of the unit as well as the working condition of all operable components of the unit. Provide instructions for all appliances and keys for all locks. Point out light switches, circuit-breaker boxes, thermostats, and any operational advice. Anticipate everything. Make sure the tenants will enjoy their move-in week without complaint. As a special touch, give your tenants a welcome basket of flowers, fruits, beverages, and snacks. If the tenants are new to the neighborhood, provide a map and a list of nearby shops, stores, schools, services, and restaurants.

Rules of Conduct

Do not just hand a list of rules to your tenants. Discuss them. Explain why the rule is important and how it adds to tenant welfare, property appearance, or upkeep. Ask the tenant to sign a copy of the rules and put it in your files with the lease, rental application, and background reports. Remind the tenant in a friendly way that the rental agreement incorporates the rules. A breach of the rules means a breach of the lease and thus triggers whatever remedies your lease provides.

Verify Move-In Condition

At the time tenants move into the property, walk through with them. If you have performed your makeready, you should find no broken windows, soiled carpets, or dirty appliances. If you do find damages that remain unrepaired, note them on your move-in checklist. Once the tenants are satisfied that they have discovered (and you have listed) every flaw, ask the tenants to sign the list to certify the move-in condition of the property. Photograph or videotape the unit on move-in day. Should a dispute over move-in condition arise, your pictures can be worth a thousand dollars.

Retain Top-Flight Residents

You've moved your tenants into the property. Now retain them as long as possible. With tenants in the property, you become a customer service representative (not a landlord). To retain tenants, keep your customers happy—until those rare exceptions force you to become a taskmaster.

Keep Tenants Informed

Don't let tenants come home to find a backhoe noisily digging up the parking lot or a pest control man spraying in their apartment. Notify and explain to tenants when anything out of the ordinary is about to happen on or within the property. Tenants don't like it when you thoughtlessly disrupt their lives or invade their privacy. Communication shows respect and concern for their welfare.

Plan Preventive Maintenance

Emergency repairs not only cost you big dollars but upset residents as well. No tenant likes a furnace that won't throw out heat, a roof that leaks, or a sink that won't drain. To eliminate these problems, plan preventive maintenance. Don't wait for things to go wrong and then react. Anticipate what can go wrong and then prevent it (or at least minimize the probabilities).

Control those seemingly minor expenses or you'll soon find they add up to major expenditures. Even though I'm a billionaire, I still look for ways to save a thousand dollars.

Expect the Unexpected

Preventive maintenance programs won't prevent every appliance malfunction or heating, ventilating, and air-conditioning breakdown. So, before they occur, set up a procedure for dealing with these problems.

For routine repairs, provide tenants a telephone number that's answered by a voice message machine. Ask your tenants to call and state their problem (you could also set up e-mail for this type of notice). Acknowledge their request within 24 hours. Repair within 72 hours (less is better). Nonresponsive landlords rank as one of the top three tenant complaints.[1] Make repairs courteously and quickly, and your tenants will sing your praises to their friends (and your future residents). For emergencies that threaten life, health, or property, provide tenants direct contact numbers (gas, roof, electrical, fire and police departments, and so on).

Enforce House Rules

Top-flight residents want you to enforce house rules consistently and without favor (or prejudice) among all tenants. Don't let those few bad apples spoil the barrel. Whether rules pertain to parking, noise, unauthorized residents (long-term "guests"), unruly pets, or mishandling of trash and garbage, you must not let violators go unnoticed (and uncorrected).

If you do, you will soon find that your good residents will move out and that you will be able to replace them with only lower-quality residents. Draft rules for the benefit of all. Then enforce them against everyone equally.

WHEN THE MARKET SUPPORTS IT, RAISE RENTS

When you raise rents, you risk losing a good tenant. Nevertheless, low rents depress your cash flows and diminish the value of your

---

[1] Noise ranks number one. Other leading complaints include high utility bills, unkempt premises, too little parking, and thoughtless (troublesome) neighbors (other tenants).

property. When your market study points toward higher rents (i.e., when you know top-flight tenants are willing to pay more than you're currently charging), raise the rents. MVP means that your target market gains a competitively superior value proposition. It does not require you to run a charitable operation.

You can alleviate tenant grumbling and nonrenewals when you offer something in return for that rent increase. How about adding covered parking, installing new carpets or appliances, installing ceiling fans, or putting in a new security system? Don't wipe out the money you will gain from the rent increase. But if you at least enhance the desirability of the property in some way the tenants appreciate, you can soothe tenant relations.

ANTICIPATE AND PREPARE FOR SPECIAL PROBLEMS

On rare occasions, even the best selected residents may run into financial difficulty. Divorce, accident, ill health, unemployment, and bankruptcy represent several common problems that hit tenants. In my early years as a landlord, I was a soft touch for sob stories—real and fictional. Several times, with previously good-paying tenants, I offered forbearance. In every case, the tenants eventually moved out and never paid the money they owed.

If your tenants need financial assistance, refer them to a charity or social services agency. Forbearance seldom leads to a win-win outcome. If they can't borrow their rent money from a bank, pawn shop, relative, or friend, then it makes no sense for you to extend them credit.

If the tenants can't pay, encourage them to leave voluntarily. You may even want to forgive some of the monies they owe you. In some instances, owners will pay the tenants to move. In nearly all cases, it's better to get rid of a tenant and accept a small loss than to drag out a bitterly fought eviction and possibly lose thousands in rent collections and attorney fees. In instances when you must evict, however, learn and precisely follow lawful procedures. If you don't dot your i's and cross your t's, the housing courts can pitch your case out and force you to refile.

Maintain the Property

In addition to preventive and corrective maintenance and repairs, schedule three other types of maintenance programs:

- *Custodial Maintenance:* Assign someone the tasks of yard care, picking up litter, and washing outside windows. Keep your property neat and clean.
- *Cosmetic Maintenance:* Periodically inspect the grounds, common areas, and rental units to freshen up their cosmetic appearance. Notice peeling paint, carpet stains, countertop burns, and other types of wear and tear. Consistent care for a property shows respect for its residents.
- *Safety and Security:* Keep your eyes open to spot problems of safety or security. Quickly repair stairs, lighting, locks, window latches, or doors. Verify that all smoke alarms work. Require your tenants to call you immediately should they discover any potential threats to health, safety, or security.

Contain costs. I willingly spend money to create the products and services my customers expect, but I don't waste money by paying more than I need to. "Why are you quibbling over a few thousand?" People ask me. Because anyone who doesn't watch their money will soon discover they have no money to watch.

Process Move-Outs Smoothly

At some point, your tenants will move on. When that time comes, process a trouble-free move-out.

Written Notice

Your lease should require your tenants to give you formal, written notice (typically 30 days, more or less) of their specific move-out date. This notice will give you time to get the word out to top-flight prospects that the area's best landlord (you!) will soon have a unit available for some lucky tenant. Early notice also gives you time to schedule work—when necessary or desirable—for improvements and repairs.

Final Walk-Through

Schedule a walk-through of the rental unit on the same day your tenants load their moving van. Compare the unit's condition to your move-in checklist, photos, or video.

With few exceptions, when I have treated my tenants with respect throughout their tenancy, when I document their damages, and when I don't try to overcharge, they honor their responsibility to cover the reasonable costs of repair.

Persistently Finds Ways to Increase Your Cash Flow

Few of us perform at the top of our game. We get lazy. We fail to notice opportunities. We again let negative self-talk and sloppy decision making rule our thought process.

Enhance perceived value. Spend money where it creates the most lasting and emotional visual effect.

Aggressively defend against these lapses. Persistently seek to better your MVP status and increase your cash flows. Set up systems to monitor competitors. Mull over tenant complaints and suggestions. Solicit feedback from prospects. Talk regularly with your network. Read idea-generating books and articles. Attend investment seminars and workshops. Enroll in Trump University courses.

Then set a firm schedule. Every 90 days, review the knowledge you have gained. Apply your insights to revise, revitalize, or maybe revolutionize your entrepreneurial MVP strategy. Thousand-dollar bills lay waiting for those who will bend over to pick them up.

To Pyramid Wealth, Trade Up

Although Donald Trump began his career with more money than most people, he nevertheless has followed the classic real estate pyramid. As his career has progressed, he has traded up to larger properties and larger deals. You should follow the same approach. Start with a small property, add value, trade up, and repeat the process. Over time, you, too, can build as much wealth as you choose.

Today's property prices dwarf those of the time when Donald Trump and I began investing. But the technique of creating value through marketing and management, then trading up, still works. I've used it. Most professional investors use it. Likewise, you can use it. Manage your properties well. Like Donald Trump, you will grow your acorns into oak trees.

13

PAY LESS THAN THE PROPERTY IS WORTH

NEGOTIATING TIPS FROM
DONALD TRUMP

Donald Trump titled his first book *The Art of the Deal* for good reason. According to Mr. Trump, deal making requires "accommodation, adjustment, diplomacy, and not the least, finesse." Negotiation requires "persuasion more than power." A "razor-sharp mind, not a bulldozer."

To succeed, Mr. Trump advises, "Think just as hard about your negotiations strategy and tactics as you would the property itself." In a nutshell, Mr. Trump stresses that to profit from negotiation, adopt these cardinal principles: (1) know yourself, (2) know the other party, and (3) prepare, prepare, prepare.

Know Yourself: What do you want from the deal? You can't get what you want unless you know what you want and how to ask for it. Do not get hung up on price alone. Look for ways to structure financing, shift risks, and solve problems.

Define your goals broadly so you can look for alternative ways to achieve them. "I always enter negotiations with Plan A, Plan B, and Plan C," says Mr. Trump. "The art of the deal is to figure out what you really want to accomplish and then persist in your creative efforts to achieve them."

Know the Other Party: "If you're building a world-class skyscraper," says Mr. Trump, "you've got to know the materials you're working with—their strengths, their weaknesses, and how they will work together to create the effect you want. This same principle applies to building a deal—only instead of working with steal, glass, marble, and brass, your materials are people."

"Don't even think about negotiating," advises Mr. Trump, "until you've learned everything about the hopes, dreams, personalities, and goals of the people you will be dealing with. If you're going to persuade people to accept your proposals, you better first learn why they're even talking to you."

"To a large extent, the art of the deal," Mr. Trump says, "is learning how to read other people. Top negotiators display a chameleon-like quality. They respond to the other party with their approach. They adapt their voice tone, body language, facts, and reasoning to the situation and the people involved." In Mr. Trump's view, only a rank amateur or egotistical smart guy rushes onto the negotiating field throwing hardballs. Savvy negotiators warm up and engage the other players.

Prepare, Prepare, Prepare: Mr. Trump likes to talk about 40 Wall Street as one of his best deals—both for what he personally accomplished (restoring a tarnished gem to brilliance) and for the profits he has earned from it. To pull it off, he prepared meticulously.

To learn more about the needs of the landowner, Mr. Trump even flew to Germany to talk with him directly, thus bypassing the bevy of gatekeepers who were blocking the deal. But in addition to knowing the building owners' and the land owners' wants, Mr. Trump knew the building, the market, and the possibilities for the property better than anyone else.

Did he gain this knowledge overnight? Hardly. He admits, "My personal and financial success from 40 Wall Street resulted all because I had my eye on that building for years. When the time came, I learned what the other parties needed, and I was prepared to act."

We negotiated a great deal on Swifton Village because we knew F.H.A. truly wanted so sell as quickly as possible.

Pay less than the property is worth, and you create immediate value for yourself. In addition, a "pay less than its worth" buying strategy sets up the potential MVP (most valued property) status for future customers. It's tough to give tenants (or buyers) a superior value proposition (and at the same time earn high profits for yourself) if you do not achieve a great buy at the time of purchase.

How to Define Great Buy

So now the question: How should you define "great buy"? When I say "pay less than a property is worth," most people conclude that means to "pay less than market value." That's one approach. But you need to envision beyond that myopic view. "Pay less than a property is worth" includes all these possibilities:

- Buy at a below-market-value price.
- Buy below use value.
- Buy below conversion value.
- Buy with below-market-costs financing.
- Buy with a below-balance payoff.
- Buy with below-average operating expenses.
- Buy with a short (discounted) payoff of liens.

Each of these approaches individually or, even better, in some combination will put you on the fast track to wealth. In one way or another, each of these approaches adds to your cash flow, builds your equity, or both.

BUY AT A BELOW-MARKET-VALUE PRICE

As mentioned in Chapter 2, many authors of "get rich in real estate" books urge their readers to find motivated sellers who are so distressed financially that they will practically give their property away to anyone who will give them a little walkaway money and pay for their moving van.

No matter how good the deal looks on paper, turn it down if your instincts say no.

Although on occasion this approach does work, it can sometimes require too much work for too little payoff. One author says to look at 100 properties, make 10 offers, and close one deal. I suspect that you can probably beat those poor odds, but the general thrust is right on. For every profitable deal, dozens of blind alleys.

Fortunately, to buy at a price less than market value, you need not limit your search to people who are going through divorce, in foreclosure or bankruptcy, or neck deep in credit card debt. You can negotiate similar attractive deals (at less trouble) with other types of property owners.

To sell at a price equal to market value, property owners need time, knowledge, and marketing expertise (or they need to employ someone who will provide the knowledge and sales know-how). In addition, market price sellers need to put up with the hassles of getting their property ready for sale, showing the property, negotiating the deal, and then worrying about whether the prospects who have written a purchase offer on the property are actually willing and able to complete the buy.

Now turn these usual requirements to achieve a market value sales price to your advantage. To find or negotiate a bargain price, identify owners who lack time, knowledge, or expertise or who want a quick, clean, no-hassle sale. Here are various types of owners (sellers) who lack the will or the ability to hold out a market value price.

Opportunistic Sellers

These owners do not value their property nearly as much as they value something else. They want to sell (the faster the better) so that they can move on with their lives. Maybe it's a retirement condo in Florida, a new job in San Diego, or a once-in-a-lifetime business venture. For these owners, the grass is greener in pastures elsewhere. Agree to a quick and sure close. These sellers will discount their price.

Don't-Wanters

In contrast to opportunistic owners who sell because they are motivated to pursue other dreams, "don't-wanters" sell because they are eager to get rid of a burden. Maybe the owner's a cranky land-lord whose ill-designed property management techniques have left him burnt out. Maybe a family moves into their new home before they sold their previous home. Now two sets of mortgage pay-ments, property taxes, and insurance premiums are eating up their monthly income. Don't-wanters need relief more than they *want* to maximize their proceeds of sale.

Emphasize how happy and free these sellers will feel once you remove this millstone from their daily trudge through life. In return, they will discount their price for you.

Unknowledgeable Sellers

Some property owners lack knowledge about the current market price of their property. I favor FSBOs (for sale by owner) and out-of-town owners (recall my purchase at a below-market-value price that you read about in Chapter 3) for these types of sellers.

On occasion, too, you'll find that real estate agents misprice properties. Fortunately for investors, some sellers choose real estate agents who are family, friends, or acquaintances to list their properties—even though those favored agents don't adequately know the property, the neighborhood, or the current market.

Recently, a house went up for sale behind a property I own. A couple days later, I phoned the listing agent for details. "Oh, we went to contract on that house the first day," she said. "We had four full-price offers." The agent had sold that house at full price but clearly not at full market value. In that market, the agent was out of touch (and the sellers lived out of town).

You can locate properties owned by out-of-towners by trolling through the billing addresses listed in the property tax assessor's records (now available online in many areas). To spot (poten-tially) mispriced agent properties, I keep a sharp eye out for "for sale" signs with real estate firms that rarely (if ever) appear in that neighborhood.

> **Originally, they wanted to sell Mar-a-Lago for $25 million. After several deals crashed, the Foundation got frustrated. I offered $8 million total—property and exquisite furnishing. With promise of a quick close, they took it.**

Windfall Gainers

Heirs inherit real estate. Do they want to try for the fast buck, or the last buck? The fast buck often seems more appealing. If the property were inherited from parents or other loved ones, for emotional reasons the heirs may not feel like hassling with a drawn out listing and sales process. If the property is mortgaged, either the estate or the heirs will need to continue making payments for PITI. Under such circumstances, the fast sale looks even better. Make these heirs a quick close, no-hassle, discount offer. They will probably accept it.

> **Before they became hot commodities, property owners sold their air rights for peanuts—they considered any sum "found money."**

You Can Pay Less Than Market Value

Owners sell for less than market value every day. Some discount price to save distress, delay, hassle, or expense. Others unknowingly give bargains. They lack firsthand knowledge, and/or they rely on supposed experts who fail to offer competent, timely advice.

Put a property discovery system in place that will bring such deals to your attention (see later discussion in this chapter). But also widen your search. Sharpen your entrepreneurial vision and negotiating skills. You can sometimes buy for less than a property is worth—even if you pay market value (or, when you must, even more than market value).

BUY BELOW USE VALUE

If you closely inspect a property, you will find ways to enhance its value. Does it include an extra large lot that permits an addition or separate unit? Does it include a garage, basement, or attic that could work as an efficiency apartment? Can you convert dead space to storage space or storage space to livable space? Can you rearrange the floor plan to improve privacy, traffic patterns, or more desirable room sizes or room counts? You can look for these and dozens of other value-creating ideas (see Chapter 10).

People pay for the benefits a property offers. Increase its usability, and you create immediate wealth. If you pay $250,000 for a property that has a market value of $300,000, you've made $50,000 (as long as you've studied the area enough to know that you're not stepping onto a down escalator). Likewise, if you pay a full market price of $300,000 for a property and immediately boost its use value by $50,000 (the present value of your extra future rent collections), you've made the same amount of gain as if you had bought at a price $50,000 below market. Either way, you've paid less than the property is worth. Pay market value or less when you can. But don't obsess over price. Focus on the total value that you can realize from the deal. Maybe the seller is not asking too much. Maybe you need to wipe clean the lens of your rose-colored glasses.

BUY BELOW CONVERSION VALUE

Neighborhoods change. Markets change. Relative prices and rent levels change. An apartment complex today, a condominium project tomorrow. A Victorian house today, an office building tomorrow.

A warehouse today, artist lofts tomorrow. A church today, a discount outlet store tomorrow.

Always look for opportunities to convert properties from an older use that no longer yields a maximum return to a use that better matches its contemporary needs. Buy at the market price of the old, reap the gain from the conversion (see Chapter 10).

Buy with Below-Market-Costs Financing

You pay for real estate in two ways: the costs of the property and the cost of the financing. Say that you can buy a $300,000 property for below-market price of $275,000. You will finance your purchase with a $250,000 loan at 7.5 percent (the going market rate) for 30 years. Alternatively, you find a seller who offers you a $300,000 property for $300,000. But you assume his current mortgage. That loan has an outstanding balance of $275,000, a fixed interest rate of 6.0 percent, and a remaining term of 27 years.

Other things equal, which deal would you choose? In this case, the mortgage assumption would give you the best outcome. Many savvy investors look not only for below-market value purchases but also for below-market interest rates.

In addition to mortgage assumptions, you can sometimes arrange for lower interest through "subject to" purchases, seller carrybacks, and seller buy-downs. With a "subject to" purchase, you agree to make the payments on the seller's mortgage, but you do not process papers with his lender. With a seller carryback, the seller agrees to let you pay him on an "installment plan." You negotiate terms and cost directly with the seller.

A seller buy-down means that the seller pays a fee to a mortgage lender. In return, the lender gives you a below-market interest rate. Sellers sometimes use buy-downs in lieu of offering their property at a lower price. (For more details, see my book *The 106 Mortgage Secrets That All Borrowers Must Learn—but Lenders Don't Tell*).

Buy with a Below-Balance Payoff

You find a laid-off, financially distressed owner who wants to clear out of his property debt free. He just wants to start over. His property has a market price of $200,000. Debts against the property include a $140,000 first mortgage, a $40,000 seller second mortgage, a $10,000 judgment lien on a credit card bill (now owned by a collection creditor), and a $6,000 mechanic's lien filed by a contractor who worked to get the property ready for sale.

The owner has made no payments on any of these debts for more than three months. This owner lacks cash and sees no hope of finding a job anytime soon in this city. He's eager to move on.

Short Payoff Possibility

At first glance, this deal looks like a nonstarter. The liens against the property ($196,000) consume nearly all its market value. With unpaid interest and legal fees adding to this balance daily, debt will overwhelm value.

As a savvy real estate entrepreneur, though, you realize that you still might be able to buy the property for less than it's worth. The owner is not the only one worried about his financial plight. The seller, the collection creditor, and the contractor are all worrying about whether they'll ever see any money from this owner.

After fooling with his front men for weeks, I went to Hyatt's top guy, Jay Pritzker. We struck a deal almost immediately. When negotiating, talk directly with the decision maker.

At a foreclosure sale (or in bankruptcy court), each of these subordinate creditors is likely to lose part or all of the money the distressed owner owes them. They have likely reached the point where some amount now seems better than little or nothing later.

So you negotiate a deal with this owner to give him what he wants: a walkaway from the property without creditors biting at his heels. You condition this offer with the provision that you reach an agreement with the creditors who hold liens against the property.

The Result

After private, persuasive discussions with each creditor, the seller who holds the $40,000 second mortgage agrees to accept $25,000, the collection firm agrees to accept $2,500, and the contractor settles for $3,000. The first-mortgage lender doesn't budge from its $140,000 claim because the bank loan mitigation manager feels that the bank would clear at least that amount from a foreclosure or bankruptcy sale.

Here are the amounts you pay to buy this property:

Creditor	Payoff	Lien amount
First mortgage	$140,000	$140,000
Seller second	$25,000	$40,000
Collection account	$2,500	$10,000
Contractor	$3,000	$6,000
Total	$170,500	196,000

You've bought the property for $29,500 less than its market value. Even when the liens against a property appear to wipe out all equity—and all possibility for a "pay less than its worth" motivated seller deal—calculate the potential for short payoffs. You still might be able to structure a deal that earns you immediate equity.

Buy with Below-Average Operating Expenses

Real estate agents and owners typically rely on the comparable sales method to price their houses, condos, and small apartment buildings. The comparable sales method (as you will see in Chapter 14) usually compares and contrasts properties according to visible features such as square footage, floor plan, condition, and lot size. The comparable sales method basically assumes that what you (or your inspector) sees is what you get.

Low Expenses Boost Value

As a savvy investor, go beyond the obvious. When you inspect a property, consider whether that property offers low expenses (property taxes, utilities, insurance, maintenance, and so on) relative to the comparable properties. Most home buyers and many investors more or less figure that operational expenses won't differ much among comparable properties. So estimates of market value often slight the actual amount of a property's operating expenses. As a result, when you find a low-expense property, you might be able to buy it for less than its really worth.

What's the Property Really Worth?

In addition to comparable sales, sharp investors use the capitalized income method to value a property. Stated simply,

$$V \text{ (value)} = \frac{\text{NOI (net operating income)}}{\text{R (capitalization rate)}}$$

where NOI equals annual rent collections less annual operating expenses and R equals the market rate of return that typical real estate investors require. For example, assume a property rents for $2,000 a month and property expenses total 40 percent of rents. The relevant cap rate equals 10 percent:

$$V = \frac{\$24,000 \text{ (rent)} \times (1 - 0.4) \text{ expenses}}{0.10 \text{ cap rate}}$$

$$V = \frac{\$14,400 \text{ (NOI)}}{0.10 \text{ (R)}}$$

$$V = \$144,000$$

The comparable sales approach also values this property within a range of $140,000 to $150,000.

Now you find a quite similar property. Comparable sales indicate a value of $140,000 to $150,000. This property could also rent for $2,000 a month ($24,000 for the year). However, unlike its comparables, this property's operating expenses total just 25 percent of rent collections vs. 40 percent for the comps (more insulation; long-life roof; energy-efficient doors, windows, and heating, ventilating, and air-conditioning (HVAC); low-maintenance exterior siding; and so on). Applying the capitalized income method, you value the property at $180,000:

$$V = \frac{\$24,000 \times (1 - 0.25)}{0.10 \text{ (R)}}$$

$$V = \frac{\$18,000 \text{ (NOI)}}{0.10 \text{ (R)}}$$

$$V = \$180,000$$

Since you can buy this property at the "comp sale" market value of around $140,000 to $150,000, you've paid less than it is really worth when used as a rental (income producing) property rather than as an owner-occupied residence.

To illustrate the point, I have simplified this example. (We will go into more detail in Chapter 14.) But the principle holds. In the world of investment real estate (all other things equal), a low-expense property is worth more than its higher-expense comparables. Yet, on occasion, you will find low-expense properties priced at less than their full value.

How to Find Good Deals

Where can you find good deals? Anywhere and everywhere. Donald Trump succeeds as a deal maker because nearly everyone who's anyone knows that Donald Trump is open to offers. From his early years, he mastered the art of self-promotion. He not only searches for opportunities but continuously invites opportunities to come to him.

> **As I was heading in from the Palm Beach airport, a pair of newly built gleaming white towers caught my eye. I looked into who owned them and discovered that a bank had just foreclosured their mortgage. I soon bought the $120 million project for $40 million. You can find good deals everywhere if you just keep your eyes and your mind open to possibilities.**

Likewise for you. Remain on active alert to discover or create deals. Get the word out. But just as important, encourage people to approach you with propositions before their deals get shopped all over town.

Competition for Properties

You can sometimes buy properties for less than their worth that have languished on the market for months—maybe even years. But today's great deals typically gain quick notice. In today's fiercely competitive market for properties, investors (or home buyers) snap up good deals within several weeks of hitting the market. Frequently, such deals go within days—or even hours.

Search Multiple Avenues

To get your share of good deals, explore multiple avenues of search and discovery. Use any or all of these methods.

Networking

Tell everyone you know. Ask if they're planning to sell or know somebody who might be thinking about it. Inquire about change-of-life possibilities (know anyone who's retiring, moving, getting divorced, in foreclosure, out of work, and so on?).

Bird Dogs

By way of their business or occupation, some people routinely learn of potential deals before others (yard care, postal delivery, lawyers [divorce, foreclosures, probate, bankruptcy], barbers, hairstylists, condo association managers, locksmiths, handymen, painters, and so on). Agree to pay a standing bounty of $500 (more or less) for each lead your bird dogs point to that results in a closed deal.

Newspapers (For-Sale Ads)

Every morning, read through the classified ads of homes for sale. Especially focus on newly placed FSBO ads and agent ads that say "new listing." Look for those common deal signals such as "motivated seller," "assumable financing," "seller will carry," "land contract," "new listing," "won't last," "must sell," and other phrases that indicate a flexible or motivated seller.

Be wary, though. Often, sellers or agents use such phrases to lure eager buyers into overpriced money traps. Nevertheless, give a call to learn whether they back their flash with substance.

Although "motivated" types of phrases signal possible good deals, unassuming ads also can offer promise. Look for plainly stated ads that state a low price (or some rare desirable feature) for that particular neighborhood. The ad might signal an unknowledgeable seller.

Newspaper (For-Rent/Lease Option)

Glance through the for-rent/lease option categories too. You might spy some wording that signals a potential deal in the making. These "sleeping sellers" are generally more flexible as to terms since they do not necessarily seek a firm sale and quick closing. Notice for-rent ads that have been running for more than two or three weeks. These ads may signal a "cranky" or otherwise disappointed landlord who is open to offer.

Newspaper (Notices)

Newspapers include more leads than the classified real estate ads. They list births, deaths, retirements, foreclosures, bankruptcies, and lawsuits. Any of these events might trigger the desire to sell a property. Many bargain hunters regularly pursue these types of leads with a letter or phone call.

Internet

Thousands of real estate Web sites list properties for sale—everything from eBay to foreclosures to FSBOs to real estate agents (multiple listing service [MLS] as well as specific firm/agent sites) to newspaper classifieds. Visit the sites that list properties in the areas that you believe promising. Keep track of the features, neighborhoods, and price ranges that appear to sell the fastest. (In addition to property searches, your local MLS site can help you stay abreast of market trends and conditions.)

Foreclosure Sales

If a defaulting property owner doesn't work out a remedy with his foreclosing lender, the property goes to sale at auction. You can either bid at the auction or try to buy the foreclosed property from the winning bidder.

Generally, you can obtain a lower price at the auction. But this method presents the greatest risks. Successful bidders at auction frequently need to resolve problems with title defects, holdover tenants or owners, and deteriorated property condition with undisclosed problems.

As an alternative to bidding at the auction yourself, buy from the winning bidder—most often the foreclosing lender or a property speculator. You'll usually pay a higher price (though not always), but the risk is less because you can inspect the property and insist that the new owner of the foreclosed property convey a deed that warrants title. (Foreclosure sales offer buyers sheriff's deeds or some other type of unwarranted title. You can read an extensive discussion of the pre- and post-foreclosure buying opportunities in my book, *Investing in Real Estate*, 5th ed., or, if you prefer audio, listen to Trump University's *The Real Estate Goldmine*).

Real Estate Agents

Make sure you establish good relations with one or more real estate agents who will hustle on your behalf. Sharp agents cull new listings each morning to find properties that match the buying criteria of their favored clients. Agents, too, learn about properties that are not yet listed but are soon to come onto the market.

It's also common for agents to deal in "pocket listings." A pocket listing refers to a juicy property that is held back from MLS until after an agent notifies preferred clients of its availability.

Describe to a savvy agent the types of properties and deals you're looking for. As long as your criteria fit within the scope of reason, you will get some hits. A savvy agent not only saves you search time but can also bring you deals that you otherwise would never hear about.

Advertise and Promote

Have you seen the "I buy ugly houses" billboards? They must generate huge numbers of hot leads. Those billboards cost a small fortune, and they're up in cities all across the country. Although you may not want to spend that kind of money on promotion, follow the same principle.

Promote and advertise yourself as a property investor. Use mailers to selected neighborhoods. Hang flyers on doorknobs. Hand out your business card to every postman, taxi driver, and waitress you see. Tell them about your bird-dog bounty. Place a magnetic sign on your car. Paint your van with your logo and telephone number. Set up a Web site. Run "wanted to buy" ads in newspapers, newsletters, and magazines. Post notices on college campus bulletin boards. If you want deals to come to you, take a tip from Donald Trump and the "I buy ugly houses" folks. Get the word out that you're ready to buy.

New Home Builders

New single-family home (or condominium) builders sometimes offer good deals at two points in their sales campaign. At the beginning of a project, builders may price below market to generate buzz about their development and to sign enough preconstruction (off-plan) contracts to satisfy the requirements of their mortgage lenders.

Near the end of a sales campaign, the builder wants to close down the sales office, eliminate overhead, and move on to the next project. At this stage, builders may cut the price to quickly sell their remaining 8 or 10 unsold units. Or they may provide sales incentives or concessions such as upgrades, homeowners' association fees paid for the first two years, below-market interest rate, or a free parking space (that otherwise would sell for $25,000). Whatever method(s) the builder uses, you receive a property at a price less than its worth.

CREATE AND NEGOTIATE A GOOD DEAL

Sometimes good deals fall into your lap. The seller (for whatever reason) asks $375,000 for a property that's clearly worth at least $425,000. You offer $360,000. The seller counters at $370,000. You moan and complain that the price is too high. You come to terms at $368,000. You're happy, the seller's happy.

That's the ideal. More often, to pay less than a property is worth, you will create and negotiate.

Exploring Possibilities

Before you negotiate price and terms, fully explore the possibilities that the property offers. Remember, paying less than a property is worth refers to numerous possibilities for gain other than a below-market price. But even with a discount price, you still want to identify all the potential that the property, neighborhood, or owner might offer.

Test the value-creating ideas of Chapters 8, 9, and 10. Only after you've figured out what the property is worth to you can you outline the type of deal that will advance you toward your $10 million net worth.

Negotiate an Agreement

Some inexperienced negotiators mistakenly believe that a skilled negotiator dips into a bag of tricks and pulls out deceptive techniques such as lowballing, weasel clauses, shotgunning (multiple random offers), "dressing to impress" (pretending to be something you're not), bad-mouthing (deflating the owners' high opinion of their homes), and eleventh-hour surprises (at the last minute before closing, insist on contract changes in your favor). One book on real estate negotiating advises, "Remember you are in a war and you must use every weapon available to win."

The tricks and deceptions may on occasion work to pull chips into your pile. But they more often backfire. Successful investors should negotiate to win an agreement that will actually close to the benefit of all parties. Working "with" creates more deals than working "against." In other words, win-win really does work.

In negotiations, look for leverage. What do you have that the other guy wants or, even better, can't do without. Don't go into a deal without first figuring out the power you possess to solve the other guy's problems.

When you negotiate win-win, you adopt a cooperative perspective. Win-win negotiators recognize that every negotiation brings forth multiple issues, priorities, and possibilities. They also recognize and respect the other party's (not opponent's) concerns, feelings, and needs. These negotiators do not push and pull along a single line of contention (e.g., price). Win-win negotiators work to create a strong, mutually beneficial agreement that all parties want to see completed. It serves little purpose to negotiate a tough deal over a period of weeks or months only to see the other party walk away and refuse to close.

Yet in your efforts to keep a deal on track, never lie down in an accommodating position while the other party hurls hardballs at you. When push comes to shove, win-win negotiators either shove back to reestablish a cooperative enterprise or they walk away with their dignity and finances intact.

Develop a Cooperative Attitude

Most important, win-win demands a cooperative approach. Bob Woolf, agent, attorney, and past negotiator for many well-known figures including Larry Bird, Larry King, and Joe Montana, says, "When I enter a negotiation, my attitude is, 'I'm going to make a deal.' I don't start with a negative thought or word. I try to foster a spirit of cooperation. I want the other party to feel that I'm forthright, cheerful, confident, and determined to reach their goals. If I'm sufficiently sensitive to the other party, I firmly believe they will be predisposed to make an agreement with me. To a degree, your attitude will become a self-fulfilling prophecy."

Bob Woolf's professional advice applies whether you are negotiating a big-time sports contract or a purchase agreement for an investment property. Act in good faith. Play by the rules of courtesy. You want to buy a property. The sellers want to sell a property. Your best chance for success comes when all parties cooperate to help each other.

Every time you communicate with a buyer, seller, or tenant, you're negotiating or setting the stage for negotiations. Plan and prepare for what result you want.

Learn as Much as You Can about the Sellers

Some lawyers and sales agents do everything they can to keep buyers and sellers away from each other. They fear that the deal might fall through because you and the seller personally clash with each other. Or you might inadvertently give away a choice bit of information that will help the other side.

Although the keep-the-buyers-and-sellers-apart sales strategy sometimes is best, as a principle, reject it. Before you make an offer, learn all you can about the sellers. What kind of people are they? Do they seem generous and open? Are they rigid and argumentative? Do they show pride in their property? Are they reluctantly moving? Are they eager to sell? Why are they selling? Have they bought another property? What are their important needs: emotional, personal, and financial? What are their worries and concerns? What deal points can you highlight that will captivate their attention and desire?

What Do the Sellers Really Want?

The sellers aren't really trying to sell a property. The sale is really a means to some other goal. The sellers will judge your offer by how well it helps them move toward what they want to achieve. That's why you must get to know the sellers. Without understanding their needs, you miss a great opportunity to find points in terms of a high-value/low-value win-win trade-off that benefit both of you.

Use negotiations to explore and discover . . . "I was just thinking about something you said. How would you feel if we could . . . "

Say the sellers previously accepted two offers that fell through because the buyers couldn't arrange financing. With these experiences in their background, the sellers don't want to be strung out again. If you can assure them that you have the resources to buy (bank statements, credit report, preapproval letter, job security), they likely will give you a lower price or other concessions.

Establish Rapport and Emotional Connection

Too frequently, investors and sellers aim their biggest negotiating gun toward price. The sellers want a higher price. You want a lower price. Antagonism and stalemate result. Steer around this trap. Meet the sellers, talk with them, and learn all you can about their perceptions, their past property experiences, their feelings, and their needs. Except for show, play it cool; avoid clashes with the sellers. Follow these guidelines:

- *Meet the Sellers as Soon as Possible:* The sooner you get a fix on who they are and what they're like, the better you can begin to map your negotiation strategy. Sellers respond more openly with information when you first look at their property. At that point, they're eager to please. They want to excite your interest. If you wait to meet them until after you've made an offer, they'll guard their admissions and concessions more tightly.
- *Get Concessions before You Begin to Negotiate:* "You're asking $325,000, is that right? Just so I can fairly compare your property to others I'm looking at, have you thought about how much less you would accept?" Or, "You're asking $325,000, right? What personal property—appliances, drapes, rugs, patio furniture, gazebo, and so on—are you planning to include?" Or maybe, "Have you considered how much financing you're willing to carry back?" By innocently suggesting concessions in this way, you're not negotiating with the sellers. You're not even asking for concessions. You're merely gathering information to

rank the sellers' property against other properties that are up for sale. Sensing that you are exploring other options, many sellers will sweeten the deal before you even write your offer.

- *Inquire, Don't Interrogate:* The way you ask your questions is far more important than the questions themselves. Phrase them as innocuously as you can. Don't intimidate, accuse, threaten, or debate. Remember Peter Falk as Columbo, the perpetually "disoriented" detective. Columbo didn't interrogate suspects. He gently probed. Use similar tactics. Encourage the easy flow of information. Don't try to extract it.

- *Establish Rapport:* Find common ground. Talk about the last Cubs game, the weather, or perhaps a shared hobby. Negotiations are about people, not money. Treat the sellers as people, not merely owners of a property that you might want to buy.

Artful negotiators (like artful developers) avoid bulldozing and clearcutting. They persuade with style rather than flatten with power.

- *Compliment, Don't Criticize:* As you inspect the sellers' property, sincerely note the beautiful grandfather clock. "Does it have an interesting history? How long have you owned it?" Comment on other belongings they seem to take pride in. What about the yard? Do the sellers have a green thumb? Can you genuinely admire their tomatoes or roses?

At this *first* meeting, put forth a cordial attitude. Establish a *relationship* bank account to draw on later when you will need it. To sharply criticize the sellers' property at this time won't loosen them up to accept a lower price. But it may turn them against you. Even though the property will need work and improvement, wait until later in the negotiations to detail the repairs and fix-up the property will need. On your first visit to the property, emphasize discovery over critique.

Don't Compromise, Conciliate

A mother hears her two children bickering at the dinner table. Each child wants the only remaining slice of pie. Tiring of this debate, the mother takes the slice, cuts it in two, and gives half to Craig and half to Chris. "There," she says, "as you get older, you've got to realize that you can't have everything you want. You must learn to compromise. Remember this as an important lesson."

This mother thought she was teaching her kids a valuable lesson. In fact, she imprinted them with one of the greatest obstacles to win-win negotiating. By splitting the difference before fully exploring her children's wants and a range of options, this mother mistakenly framed her kids' debate along a single continuum. Compromise simply meant deciding how to split the piece of pie.

Look for Ways to Make a Pie Bigger

Had the mother framed the problem multidimensionally, more than likely she could have figured out a better solution. What if Chris preferred the crust and Craig preferred the filling? What if the children shared a television set and each preferred different programs? What if the children shared after-dinner cleanup responsibilities? What if the children had money from an allowance? What if Chris didn't want the pie but simply liked to torment Craig?

Had the mother recognized a range of wants, trade-offs, and outcomes, she may have produced results more satisfying (or just) for both children. The true art of the deal does not depend on one's readiness to strike a compromise. It depends on seeing beyond a single either/or issue. Thoughtful and exploratory conciliation beats an everyone-loses (or anyone-loses) compromise.

Compromise Provokes Extremes

People who negotiate to compromise typically open with offers at the extreme. If you believe the sellers will split the difference, it's to your advantage to offer $550,000 for a property that's worth $650,000. Should the sellers agree to meet you halfway, they will sell you the property for $600,000.

Few sellers are that obliging. The tactic of bid low and compromise is too familiar to work effectively. As negotiating expert Herb Cohen likes to emphasize, "A tactic perceived is no tactic at all." You're more likely to negotiate successfully if you use a larger pie pan. Broaden your knowledge of wants, needs, trade-offs, and possibilities. To paraphrase Emerson, "Foolish compromises are the hobgoblins of little minds."

Learn the Sellers' Reasons and Reference Points

When the sellers say, "This property is worth at least $425,000," learn their reference points. Why do they think $425,000 represents bottom dollar? When the sellers say, "We need at least $425,000," find out why. When the sellers say, "We couldn't afford to carry back financing, we need every net dollar in cash," find out why. No matter what objection they raise to your proposal, never accept it as the final word. Find the real underlying reasons and the supposed factual foundation that the sellers are building on to support their decision (or their counterproposal).

Fast-talking sales agents deal with objections like a steamroller. They just charge forward and try to flatten the prospect's reluctance without bothering to slow down, let alone, stop, look, and listen. In contrast, do not *overcome* objections by the methods taught in those high-pressure sales training classes. Try to correct, alleviate, or eliminate the sellers' misperceptions through better understanding.

If it turns out that the sellers' facts or perceptions make sense, work toward resolve. A confused mind always says no. To get a yes, assuage the sellers' real concerns.

Use an Agent as an Intermediary but Negotiate for Yourself

Writing in *Real Estate Today*, a national trade magazine for real estate agents, sales agent Sal Greer tells of an offer he received on one of his listings. Sal says that after receiving the purchase offer from a *buyer's agent*, this agent told Sal, "This is their [first] offer, but I know my buyers will go up to $150,000."

"Of course," Sal adds, "I told my sellers that information, and we were pleased with the outcome of the transaction."

Never let your real estate agent or lawyer control your negotiations. Do not give your agent information you do not want the other side to learn. Do not let on to your agent that you're willing to pay a higher price than your first offer. Use your agent as a fact finder and intermediary. But guard your emotions, confidences, and intentions.

Some investors mistakenly rely too heavily on their agents or lawyers to actually come up with the terms of their offer and then carry out their negotiations. These investors will ask their agents, "What price do you think I should offer? What's the most you think I should pay? Will the sellers concede points or agree to carryback financing?" The buyers then follow whatever the agent recommends.

Control the lawyers. Left unleashed, their attacks can kill good deals.

When you abdicate your negotiating responsibilities, you set yourself up for all the decision-making "expert advice" mistakes discussed in Chapter 3.

Leave Something on the Table

Negotiating expert Bob Woolf says, "There isn't any contract I have negotiated where I didn't feel I could have gone for more money or an additional benefit." Why "leave money on the table?" Because skilled negotiators know that "the deal's not over until it's over." Push too hard, and you draw resentment and hostility from the other party. Even if they've signed a contract, they'll start thinking of all the ways they can get out of it. Worse, if you stumble on the way to closing, they won't help you up. They'll just kick dirt in your face.

Especially in the purchase of real estate—where emotions run strong—you're better off leaving something on the table. The purchase agreement sets only the first stage of your negotiations. Later, problems might arise with property inspections, appraisal, financing, possession date, closing date, surveys, zoning, building permits, or any number of other things. Without goodwill, trust, and cooperation, unpleasant setbacks on the way to closing can throw your agreement into a deal-killing dispute.

Deal Points

Of course, you will negotiate price, but use price as just one chip, not your entire pile. Even simple purchase agreements will include at least 8 or 10 other critical deal points. As you negotiate, look for high-value/low-value trade-offs that benefit you and the seller. What can you offer in trade for a lower price? What can the seller offer you that could tempt you to concede a higher price than you otherwise would agree to pay?

1. *Terms:* Will the seller offer owner-assisted financing? If so, how much up-front cash? What interest rate? What amount of monthly payments? Exactly what type of financing assistance (lease option, lease purchase, land contract, first mortgage, second mortgage, and so on)?
2. *Closing Costs:* In most areas, custom dictates who pays what settlement expenses. But negotiation can override custom. With settlement costs upward of $5,000, smart investors put these amounts on the table for discussion.
3. *Earnest-Money Deposit:* To show your commitment to a deal, you will bind your offer with an earnest-money deposit. How much? That's subject to negotiation.

4. *Repair Allowance:* In lieu of (or along with) a price reduction, you can negotiate a repair allowance for some of the fix-up work you plan for the property.

5. *Personal Property:* Would you like the seller to include window air conditioners, appliances, or other personal property in the sale? Write them into your offer.

6. *Financing Contingencies:* If the seller does not provide all your financing, you will probably include a financing contingency in your offer. This clause will give you a specified amount of time to raise the money you will need to close the deal. It will also set the terms, such as interest rate, loan-to-value (LTV) ratio, down payment amount, and so on, that a lender must offer you. Otherwise, you're released from the agreement and entitled to a return of your earnest money.

7. *Inspection Contingencies:* Get the property professionally inspected for physical condition, termites, and environmental hazards. How long do you have to complete these inspections? Who pays how much for any unanticipated or previously unknown problems? Under what scenarios can you withdraw from the agreement without obligation? Negotiation touches on all these issues.

8. *Closing Date:* To gain a bargain price, many investors offer a fast closing. Does your seller voice a strong preference?

9. *Possession Date:* Generally, sellers relinquish possession on or around the date of closing. Sometimes, though, you may want a delayed closing with early possession (such as with a lease purchase or lease option). Or, alternatively, the sellers may want to seal the deal but hold on to the property until, say, the school year ends, their new home is ready for them to move into, or they locate a replacement property for a Section 1031 tax-deferred exchange.

10. *Warranties:* Is the seller providing you a warranty for components such as the roof, HVAC, or appliances? What exactly do the warranties cover, for what amounts, and for what period of time?

Every purchase-sale agreement addresses many significant deal points. To negotiate entrepreneurially, never view any one of these issues as separate from the others. Instead, find a combination that will work for you and the other party.

Reduce Seller Anxiety

Often sellers will agree to accept a "pro-buyer" agreement if you show them that you're a solid buyer and that the deal will actually close. To persuade sellers and reduce their anxiety, draw from the following eight negotiating tactics:

1. Increase the amount of your earnest-money deposit.
2. Produce a preapproval letter from a mortgage lender to reveal your bank balances and credit score to assure sellers that you possess the money and credit to do the deal.
3. If you're paying cash or making a large down payment, emphasize that fact. Cash counts. If you've got it, use it to boost the credibility of your position.
4. Emphasize the strength of your character, stability in your job and community, investment experience, and other factors that prove you're able and willing to quickly close the deal.
5. Avoid weasel clauses in your offer. A weasel clause is any clause that lets you weasel out of or easily escape from a contract without obligation. One of the easiest and most obvious weasel clauses states, "This offer is subject to the approval of my attorney." If you need to consult an attorney, do it before you begin negotiations. (In some states, by custom, attorneys routinely get involved in negotiating property purchase agreements. Nevertheless, the same advice holds. The firmer your offer, the more likely the sellers will treat you as a serious buyer and make concessions toward an agreement.)
6. Avoid indefinite contingency clauses such as "Offer subject to raising $10,000 from my business partners" or "Subject

to locating a 1031 replacement property." Sometimes home owners write into their offer, "Subject to the sale of our current home." Clauses like these raise doubts and increase anxiety. Load your contract with "ifs, ands, or buts," and sellers will hesitate to accept it.

7. When you write contingency clauses into your offer, make them definite and short term: "Buyer will secure a property inspection report within five days," "Buyer agrees to submit mortgage loan application within 48 hours," or "Sellers are released from obligation if buyers do not produce a letter of mortgage credit approval within three days." These clauses show that you're not going to drag your feet through the transaction.

8. Make your contingency clauses realistic. Don't condition your purchase on finding mortgage money at 6.0 percent if market rates are at 7.5 percent. Don't require a 27-year-old property to be free of all defects. The firmer your offer, the more willing the sellers may be to accept a price that's less than their property is worth.

Plan your offer with no more escape hatches than you need (but no fewer either). Some sellers do trade off price and terms for the peace of mind of a near-certain sale. That's why buyers who pay cash nearly always gain more seller concessions than those investors who load their contracts with weasel clauses.

Increasingly, sellers expect you to line up your ducks before you start shooting. Remember, you will compete for the best deals with other sharp, entrepreneurial investors. While you're fiddling with contingencies and thinking things over, someone else will grab the prize.

When you find a property that you think you can buy for less than it's worth, put it under contract immediately. Use short-fuse contingencies when prudence dictates. But otherwise, come to the negotiating table prepared to deal.

14

How to Value Properties

At the right price, I'd buy it.

You've discovered how to define, discover, and negotiate great deals. Now you'll learn how to value those deals. We'll begin with a discussion of market value and then illustrate several other valuation techniques that investors also rely on to guide their decisions.

The Uniform Residential Appraisal Report

Although you should never use market value as your sole decision guide, refer to it as one major data point. To estimate the market value of houses, townhouses, and condominiums, most lenders, investors, and appraisers use a form similar to that shown in Figure 14.1.

The two leading sources of mortgage money in the United States, Freddie Mac and Fannie Mae, have both approved this form and are responsible for its widespread use. Lenders and investors in countries other than the United States also follow a similar appraisal process. No matter where a property is located, the principles of market valuation remain the same.

We will now go through each of the major sections of this appraisal form.

A Word of Warning

Beware: Too many lenders, home buyers, and investors merely look at an appraisal's value conclusion. But value conclusions are worth no more than the accuracy of the data and the quality of the reasoning that support them. Regrettably, experience proves that appraisals often err in facts, reasoning, and judgment.

Regardless of whether you're doing your own appraisal or reviewing the work of an appraiser, critically examine all input data and question all inferences and conclusions.

Uniform Residential Appraisal Report   File

The purpose of this summary appraisal report is to provide the lender/client with an accurate, and adequately supported, opinion of the market value of the subject property.

Property Address	City	State	Zip Code

S U B J E C T

Property Address		City		State	Zip Code
Borrower	Owner of Public Record			County	
Legal Description					
Assessor's Parcel #		Tax Year		R.E. Taxes $	
Neighborhood Name		Map Reference		Census Tract	
Occupant ☐ Owner ☐ Tenant ☐ Vacant	Special Assessments $		☐ PUD	HOA $	☐ per year ☐ per month
Property Rights Appraised ☐ Fee Simple ☐ Leasehold ☐ Other (describe)					
Assignment Type ☐ Purchase Transaction ☐ Refinance Transaction ☐ Other (describe)					
Lender/Client		Address			

Is the subject property currently offered for sale or has it been offered for sale in the twelve months prior to the effective date of this appraisal? ☐ Yes ☐ No

Report data source(s) used, offering price(s), and date(s).

C O N T R A C T

I ☐ did ☐ did not analyze the contract for sale for the subject purchase transaction. Explain the results of the analysis of the contract for sale or why the analysis was not performed.

Contract Price $ Date of Contract   Is the property seller the owner of public record? ☐ Yes ☐ No Data Source(s)

Is there any financial assistance (loan charges, sale concessions, gift or downpayment assistance, etc.) to be paid by any party on behalf of the borrower? ☐ Yes ☐ No

If Yes, report the total dollar amount and describe the items to be paid.

Note: Race and the racial composition of the neighborhood are not appraisal factors.

N E I G H B O R H O O D

Neighborhood Characteristics			One-Unit Housing Trends			One-Unit Housing		Present Land Use %	
Location ☐ Urban ☐ Suburban ☐ Rural			Property Values ☐ Increasing ☐ Stable ☐ Declining			PRICE	AGE	One-Unit	%
Built-Up ☐ Over 75% ☐ 25-75% ☐ Under 25%			Demand/Supply ☐ Shortage ☐ In Balance ☐ Over Supply			$ (000)	(yrs)	2-4 Unit	%
Growth ☐ Rapid ☐ Stable ☐ Slow			Marketing Time ☐ Under 3 mths ☐ 3-6 mths ☐ Over 6 mths			Low		Multi-Family	%
Neighborhood Boundaries						High		Commercial	%
						Pred.		Other	%

Neighborhood Description

Market Conditions (including support for the above conclusions)

S I T E

Dimensions	Area	Shape	View
Specific Zoning Classification	Zoning Description		

Zoning Compliance ☐ Legal ☐ Legal Nonconforming (Grandfathered Use) ☐ No Zoning ☐ Illegal (describe)

Is the highest and best use of the subject property as improved (or as proposed per plans and specifications) the present use? ☐ Yes ☐ No If No, describe

Utilities	Public	Other (describe)		Public	Other (describe)	Off-site Improvements--Type	Public	Private
Electricity	☐	☐	Water	☐	☐	Street	☐	☐
Gas	☐	☐	Sanitary Sewer	☐	☐	Alley	☐	☐

FEMA Special Flood Hazard Area ☐ Yes ☐ No FEMA Flood Zone   FEMA Map #   FEMA Map Date

Are the Utilities and off-site improvements typical for the market area? ☐ Yes ☐ No If No, describe

Are there any adverse site conditions or external factors (easements, encroachments, environmental conditions, land uses, etc.)? ☐ Yes ☐ No If Yes, describe

I M P R O V E M E N T S

General Description	Foundation	Exterior Description materials/condition	Interior materials/condition
Units ☐ One ☐ One with Accessory Unit	☐ Concrete Slab ☐ Crawl Space	Foundation Walls	Floors
# of Stories	☐ Full Basement ☐ Partial Basement	Exterior Walls	Walls
Type ☐ Det. ☐ Att. ☐ S-Det./End Unit	Basement Area sq. ft.	Roof Surface	Trim/Finish
☐ Existing ☐ Proposed ☐ Under Const.	Basement Finish %	Gutters & Downspouts	Bath Floor
Design (Style)	☐ Outside Entry/Exit ☐ Sump Pump	Window Type	Bath Wainscot
Year Built	Evidence of ☐ Infestation	Storm Sash/Insulated	Car Storage ☐ None
Effective Age (Yrs)	☐ Dampness ☐ Settlement	Screens	☐ Driveway # of Cars
Attic ☐ None	Heating ☐ FWA ☐ HWBB ☐ Radiant	Amenities ☐ Woodstove(s) #	Driveway Surface
☐ Drop Stair ☐ Stairs	☐ Other Fuel	☐ Fireplace(s) # ☐ Fence	☐ Garage # of Cars
☐ Floor ☐ Scuttle	Cooling ☐ Central Air Conditioning	☐ Patio/Deck ☐ Porch	☐ Carport # of Cars
☐ Finished ☐ Heated	☐ Individual ☐ Other	☐ Pool ☐ Other	☐ Att. ☐ Det. ☐ Built-in

Appliances ☐ Refrigerator ☐ Range/Oven ☐ Dishwasher ☐ Disposal ☐ Microwave ☐ Washer/Dryer ☐ Other (describe)

Finished area above grade contains: Rooms   Bedrooms   Bath(s)   Square Feet of Gross Living Area Above Grade

Additional features (special energy efficient items, etc.).

Describe the condition of the property (including needed repairs, deterioration, renovations, remodeling, etc.).

Are there any physical deficiencies or adverse conditions that affect the livability, soundness, or structural integrity of the property? ☐ Yes ☐ No If Yes, describe

Does the property generally conform to the neighborhood (functional utility, style, condition, use, construction, etc.)? ☐ Yes ☐ No If No, describe

Figure 14.1

(continued)

237

Uniform Residential Appraisal Report

File #

There are _____ comparable properties currently offered for sale in the subject neighborhood ranging in price from $ _____ to $ _____
There are _____ comparable sales in the subject neighborhood within the past twelve months ranging in sale price from $ _____ to $ _____

FEATURE	SUBJECT	COMPARABLE SALE # 1		COMPARABLE SALE # 2		COMPARABLE SALE # 3	
Address							
Proximity to Subject							
Sale Price	$		$		$		$
Sale Price/Gross Liv.Area	$ sq. ft.	$ sq. ft.		$ sq. ft.		$ sq. ft.	
Data Source(s)							
Verification Source(s)							
VALUE ADJUSTMENTS	DESCRIPTION	DESCRIPTION	+(-) $ Adjustment	DESCRIPTION	+(-) $ Adjustment	DESCRIPTION	+(-) $ Adjustment
Sale or Financing							
Concessions							
Date of Sale/Time							
Location							
Leasehold/Fee Simple							
Site							
View							
Design (Style)							
Quality of Construction							
Actual Age							
Condition							
Above Grade	Total Bdrms. Baths	Total Bdrms. Baths		Total Bdrms. Baths		Total Bdrms. Baths	
Room Count							
Gross Living Area	sq. ft.	sq. ft.		sq. ft.		sq. ft.	
Basement & Finished Rooms Below Grade							
Functional Utility							
Heating/Cooling							
Energy Efficient Items							
Garage/Carport							
Porch/Patio/Deck							
Net Adjustment (Total)		☐ + ☐ -	$	☐ + ☐ -	$	☐ + ☐ -	$
Adjusted Sale Price of Comparables		Net Adj. % Gross Adj. %	$	Net Adj. % Gross Adj. %	$	Net Adj. % Gross Adj. %	$

(Left margin vertical text: SALES COMPARISON APPROACH)

I ☐ did ☐ did not research the sale or transfer history of the subject property and comparable sales. If not, explain

My research ☐ did ☐ did not reveal any prior sales or transfers of the subject property for the three years prior to the effective date of this appraisal.

Data source(s)

My research ☐ did ☐ did not reveal any prior sales or transfers of the comparable sales for the year prior to the date of sale of the comparable sale.

Data source(s)

Report the results of the research and analysis of the prior sale or transfer history of the subject property and comparable sales (report additional prior sales on page 3).

ITEM	SUBJECT	COMPARABLE SALE # 1	COMPARABLE SALE # 2	COMPARABLE SALE # 3
Date of Prior Sale/Transfer				
Price of Prior Sale/Transfer				
Data source(s)				
Effective Date of Data source(s)				

Analysis of prior sale or transfer history of the subject property and comparable sales

Summary of Sales Comparison Approach

Indicated value by Sales Comparision Approach $

(Left margin vertical text: RECONCILIATION)

Indicated value by: Sales Comparison Approach $ _____ Cost Approach(if developed) $ _____ Income Approach (if developed) $ _____

This appraisal is made☐ "as is", ☐ subject to completion per plans and specifications on the basis of a hypothetical condition that the improvements have been completed, ☐ subject to the following repairs or alterations on the basis of a hypothetical condition that the repairs or alterations have been completed, or ☐ subject to the following required inspection based on the extraordinary assumption that the condition or deficiency does not require alteration or repair:

Based on a complete visual inspection of the interior and exterior areas of the subject property, defined scope of work, statement of assumptions and limiting conditions, and appraiser's certification, my (our) opinion of the market value, as defined, of the real property that is the subject of this report is
$ _____ as of _____, which is the date of inspection and the effective date of this appraisal.

Figure 14.1 *(continued)*

(continued)

238

A D D I T I O N A L   C O M M E N T S

(blank ruled lines for additional comments)

COST APPROACH TO VALUE (not required by Fannie Mae)

Provide adequate information for the lender/client to replicate the below cost figures and calculations.

Support for the opinion of site value (summary of comparable land sales or other methods for estimating site value)

ESTIMATED ☐ REPRODUCTION OR ☐ REPLACEMENT COST NEW	OPINION OF SITE VALUE .... =$
Source of cost data	Dwelling Sq. Ft. @ $ .... =$
Quality rating from cost service Effective date of cost data	Sq. Ft. @ $ .... =$
Comments on Cost Approach (gross living area calculations, depreciation, etc.)	Garage/Carport Sq. Ft. @ $ .... =$
	Total Estimate of Cost-New .... =$
	Less Physical Functional External
	Depreciation =$ ( )
	Depreciated Cost of Improvements.. =$
	"As-is" Value of Site Improvements.. =$
Estimated Remaining Economic Life (HUD and VA only) Years	Indicated Value By Cost Approach .... =$

INCOME APPROACH TO VALUE (not required by Fannie Mae)

Estimated Monthly Market Rent $ X Gross Rent Multiplier   = $ Indicated Value by Income Approach

Summary of Income Approach (including support for market rent and GRM)

PROJECT INFORMATION FOR PUDs (if applicable)

Is the developer/builder in control of the Homeowners' Association (HOA)? ☐ Yes ☐ No   Unit type(s) ☐ Detached ☐ Attached

Provide the following information for PUDs ONLY if the developer/builder is in control of the HOA and the subject property is an attached dwelling unit.

Legal name of project

Total number of phases   Total number of units   Total number of units sold
Total number of units rented   Total number of units for sale   Data source(s)

Was the project created by the conversion of an existing building(s) into a PUD? ☐ Yes ☐ No   If Yes, data of conversion

Does the project contain any multi-dwelling units? ☐ Yes ☐ No   Data source(s)

Are the units, common elements, and recreation facilities complete? ☐ Yes ☐ No   If No, describe the status of completion.

Are the common elements leased to or by the Homeowners' Association? ☐ Yes ☐ No   If Yes, describe the rental terms and options.

Describe common elements and recreational facilities

Figure 14.1 _(continued)_   _(continued)_

This report form is designed to report an appraisal of a one-unit property or a one-unit property with an accessory unit; including a unit in a planned unit development (PUD). This report form is not designed to report an appraisal of a manufactured home or a unit in a condominium or cooperative project.

This appraisal report is subject to the following scope of work intended use, intended user, definition of market value, statement of assumptions and limiting conditions, and certifications. Modifications, additions, or deletions to the intended use, intended user, definition of market value, or assumptions and limiting conditions are not permitted. The appraiser may expand the scope of work to include any additional research or analysis necessary based on the complexity of this appraisal assignment. Modifications or deletions to the certifications are also not permitted. However, additional certifications that do not constitute material alterations to this appraisal report, such as those required by low or those related to the appraiser's continuing education or membership in an appraisal organization, are permitted.

SCOPE OF WORK: The scope of work for this appraisal is defined by the complexity of this appraisal assignement and the reporting requirements of this appraisal report form, including the following definition of market value, statement of assumptions and limiting conditions, and certifications. The appraiser must, at a minimum: (1) perform a complete visual inspection of the interior and exterior areas of the subject property, (2) inspect the neighborhood, (3) inspect each of the comparable sales from at least the street, (4) research, verify, and analyze data from reliable public and/or private sources, and (5) report his or her analysis, opinions, and conclusions in this appraisal report.

INTENDED USE: The intended use of this appraisal report is for the lender/client to evaluate the property that is the subject of this appraisal for a mortgage finance transaction.

INTENDED USER: The intended user of this appraisal report is the lender/client.

DEFINITION OF MARKET VALUE: The most probable price which a property should bring in a competitive and open market under all conditions requisite to a fair sale, the buyer and seller, each acting prudently, knowledgeably and assuming the price is not affected by undue stimulus. Implicit in this definition is the consummation of a sale as of a specified date and the passing of title from seller to buyer under conditions whereby; (1) buyer and seller are typically motivated; (2) both parties are well informed or well advised, and each acting in what he or she considers his or her own best interest; (3) a reasonable time is allowed for exposure in the open market; (4) payment is made in terms of cash in U. S. dollars or in terms of financial arrangements comparable thereto; and (5) the price represents the normal consideration for the property sold unaffected by special or creative financing or sales concessions* granted by anyone associated with the sale.

*Adjustments to the comparables must be made for special or creative financing or sales concessions. No adjustments are necessary for those costs which are normally paid by sellers as a result of tradition or law in a market area; these costs are readily identifiable since the seller pays these costs in virtually all sales transactions. Special or creative financing adjustments can be made to the comparable property by comparisons to financing terms offered by a third party institutional lender that is not already involved in the property or transaction. Any adjustment should not be calculated on a mechanical dollar for dollar cost of the financing or concession but the dolar amount of any adjustment should approximate the market's reaction to the financing or concessions based on the appraiser's judgment.

STATEMENT OF ASSUMPTIONS AND LIMITING CONDITIONS: The appraiser's certification in this report is subject to the following assumptions and limiting conditions:

1. The appraiser will not be responsible for matters of a legal nature that affect either the property being appraised or the title to it, except for information that he or she became aware of during the research involved in performing this appraisal. The appraiser assumes that the title is good and marketable and will not render any opinions about the title.

2. The appraiser has provided a sketch in this appraisal report to show the approximate dimensions of the improvements. The sketch is included only to assist the reader in visualizing the property and understanding the appraiser's determination of its size.

3. The appraiser has examined the available flood maps that are provided by the Federal Emergency Management Agency (or other data sources) and has noted in this appraisal report whether any portion of the subject site is located in an identified Special Flood Hazard Area. Because the appraiser is not a surveyor, he or she makes no guarantes, express or implied, regarding this determination.

4. The appraiser will not give testimony or appear in court because he or she made an appraisal of the property in question, unless specific arrangements to do so have been mede beforehand, or as otherwise required by law.

5. The appraiser has noted in this appraisal report any adverse conditions (such as needed repairs, deterioration, the presence of hazardous wastes, toxic substances, etc.) observed during the inspection of the subject property or that he or she became aware of during the research involved in performing this appraisal. Unless otherwise stated in this appraisal report, the appraiser has no knowledge of any hidden or unapparent physical deficiencies or adverse conditions of the property (such as, but not limited to, needed repairs, deterioration, the presence of hazardous wastes, toxic substances, adverse environmental conditions, etc.) that would make the property less valuable, and has assumed that there are no such conditions and makes no guarantees or warranties, express or implied. The appraiser will not be responsible for any such conditions that do exist or for any engineering or testing that might be required to discover whether such conditions exist. Because the appraiser is not an expert in the field of environmental hazards, this appraisal report must not be considered as an environmental assessment of the property.

6. The appraiser has based his or her appraisal report and valuation conclusion for an appraisal that is subject to satisfactory completion, repairs, or alterations on the assumption that the completion, repairs, or alterations of the subject property will be performed in a professional manner.

Figure 14.1 *(continued)*

How to Critique a Market Value Appraisal

In the following pages, we won't be able to cover every detail of information that the form actually requires. We will, though, discuss each section of the report and highlight frequent sources of mistakes and questionable judgments.

SUBJECT PROPERTY

This first section sets up the appraisal problem. Most of this information is relatively straightforward. Nevertheless, it still pays to verify for accuracy. Note, too, the importance of property rights.

Appraisals of real estate need to consider if the title to the property can be conveyed free of any liens, clouds, or encumbrances (such as easements or leases). Remember, you're not just buying land and buildings. You're buying the legal rights that govern use, occupancy, transfer, redevelopment, and so on. Most professionally prepared appraisals generally *assume* that property rights present no significant issues. Do not rely on such assumptions. Consult a title company or an attorney who specializes in property law.

CONTRACT

Most lenders lend against the contract price *or* the market value of a property—whichever is less. Say you find a great bargain. You negotiate a price of $160,000 for a property that's valued at $200,000. You figure that with an 80 percent loan-to-value (LTV) ratio (80% × $200,000), the bank will loan you your full purchase price of $160,000. Good idea, but most banks would loan you only $128,000 (80% × $160,000). That's why banks require knowledge of the contract price.

241

Never Lie to a Lender

To get around this issue, some dishonest buyers do a side deal with the sellers and draft a second contract that lists a $200,000 price and then shows that false contract to the bank. Such a deception qualifies as bank fraud. Do not do it.

Never lie to a lender about your true contract price or any other fact material to a loan application or loan agreement. (The famous lobbyist Jack Abramoff was just sentenced to federal prison for six years for deceptive borrowing.)

Seller Concessions

Sometimes buyers agree to pay sellers an above-market price. In exchange, sellers may offer to pay the buyer's down payment, mortgage fees, or closing costs. Or maybe the sellers include an unusually large amount of furniture, household furnishings, and appliances with the sale. In these instances or any similar instances where sellers provide valuable concessions to their buyers, the bank wants to know the property's market value, not merely the contract price. Market value will set the amount for calculating the bank's LTV ratio.

NEIGHBORHOOD

First, note that federal law does not permit appraisers to discuss or become influenced by the existing or evolving racial composition of a neighborhood. Therefore, no professionally prepared appraisal report will ever mention racial neighborhood demographics.

Neighborhood Supply, Demand, and Price Ranges

Otherwise, appraisal reports briefly refer to the types and uses of properties in the neighborhood, the prevailing price ranges, and whether the number of "for sale" and "for rent" properties are stable, increasing, or decreasing.

As an investor, pay close attention to these types of market trend indicators. Whereas market value appraisals focus primarily on the present, you want to envision the future.

Economic Base and Neighborhood Effects

Because of their emphasis on the present, residential appraisals not only slight neighborhood trends but also omit any thorough review of an area's economic base, employment, and future growth or decline. Again, as an investor, you must research and investigate these topics in much more depth.

Just as important, assess how changes in jobs, transportation arteries, and growth patterns within a total metro area will affect specific neighborhoods. Even in declining areas, some neighborhoods might prosper. And even in growth areas, some neighborhoods might suffer deterioration and decline. Market value appraisals rarely point to these future developments.

SITE

In many urban areas, site value can total 30 to 60 percent (sometimes more) of a property's market value. Give this part of your appraisal careful consideration. First, stake out and walk the site boundaries. Measure the dimensions. You want to learn the site area both visually and by size.

Zoning and Land-Use Laws

As you learned from Chapter 8, zoning and land-use laws can regulate properties in dozens of different ways. Knowing the ins and outs of these rules can open the door to many creative opportunities. Or they may shut out your otherwise brilliantly conceived entrepreneurial plans. Learn these laws in detail, not just by broad classification (e.g., residential, commercial, industrial, agricultural, and so on).

A market value appraisal may or may not accurately note whether a property adequately conforms to applicable zoning and building regulations. But few appraisals would spell out how you could take advantage of such laws (including the possibility of rezoning) to add value to the property.

Utilities

Contrary to what city slickers might believe, not all sites are serviced by all utilities. I know an experienced investor who bought a house without realizing that it lacked a sewer connection and thus used a septic tank for waste disposal. Other things being equal, the lack of a sewer connection materially reduces a property's value.

Don't make the mistake of that investor. Verify the gas, water, sewer, cable, security, and Internet connections to the property. Although appraisals seldom mention utility costs per se, these expenses can add or detract from a property's value. So, in addition to availability, anticipate how much these costs will run. Consult the relevant service providers for past usage rates and billing amounts.

IMPROVEMENTS

In real estate lingo, improvements include not only the building(s) but also sidewalks, landscaping, pools, tennis courts, fencing, basements, storage sheds, fireplaces, appliances, decks, patios, porches, driveways, garages, and so on. To value a property, carefully itemize and assess the quality of all site and building improvements.

Also note square footage, room counts, closets, floor plan, energy efficiency, insulation, windows (energy, design, safety, and usability), architectural design, livability, age, and condition. Every one of these details can prove important to a property's value and your efforts to create a property your tenants or buyers will value most highly. Accordingly, all these improvement (and neighborhood) details set the stage for the three important residential valuation techniques.

RESIDENTIAL VALUATION TECHNIQUES

To best estimate market value, appraise the property from three perspectives:

1. *The Comparables Sales Approach:* This valuation technique compares the features and recent selling prices of similar properties to the subject property (see Figure 14.2).
2. *The Cost Approach:* This method calculates the cost you would have to pay to reconstruct the property (plus land value) today and then subtracts an amount for depreciation (see Figure 14.3).
3. *The Income Approach:* This appraisal method capitalizes the net rental income stream of a property and converts that income into a market value estimate (see Figure 14.4).

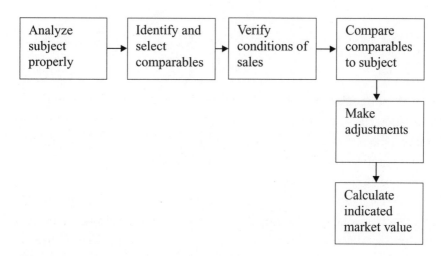

Figure 14.2 Comparative Sales Approach.

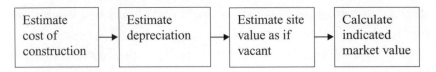

Figure 14.3 Cost Approach.

After you figure the indicated market values with each of these three approaches, you next derive a market value range for the property and decide your best estimate of value (see Figure 14.5). Generally, you will emphasize the comp sales approach for houses, townhouses, co-ops, and condominiums, and the income approach for multiunit residential properties as well as office buildings and shopping centers. In practice, appraisers rely on the cost approach primarily as a check (or verification of value) on the comp sales and income approaches.

Special Note: As mentioned in an earlier chapter, the cost approach can also help you determine future price increases or decreases. (See the later discussion of the cost approach for income properties.)

Recall that when properties sell for prices that substantially exceed their replacement costs, builders often rush to construct new properties. Unfortunately, this stampede to earn

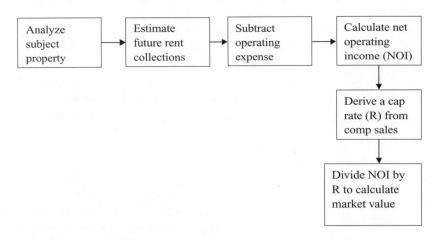

Figure 14.4 Capitalized Income Approach.

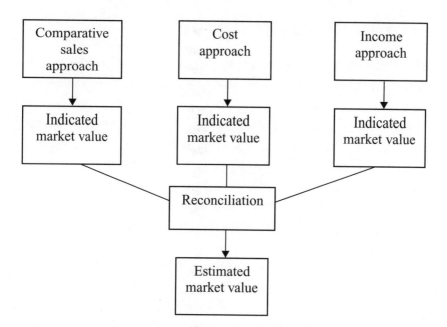

Figure 14.5   Three Approaches to Market Value.

extraordinary profits often brings about losses as newly built supply temporarily outpaces demand. To work off excess inventories of unsold (or unrented) properties, builders slash prices and rents and offer generous buyer (renter) incentives and concessions (e.g., upgrades, below-market financing, two months of free rent, $99 move-in specials, and so on).

In contrast, when properties sell for substantially less than their cost of construction (as in cases of economic recession or oversupply), builders withdraw from the market. Eventually, a growing economy creates more jobs and higher incomes. Excess "for sale" and "for rent" properties are absorbed. New buyers and renters compete for a dwindling number of available units. They bid prices and rents up.

For these reasons, savvy entrepreneurial investors always track replacement costs, builder profits, builder inventories of unsold (unrented) properties, and other market trends. Again, I emphasize evaluating the past and the present but also gazing into your crystal ball and envisioning the future.

The Comparables Sales Approach

Refer now to page 2 of Figure 14.1, where you can see the specific information that appraisers incorporate into their comp sale value estimates.

The comp sales method works best when you closely inspect and itemize the features of the subject property and the comparable properties. That's why I encourage you to look at every property that comes up for sale in the area where you would like to buy. Record their features in detail. Take photographs. Write out comments and notes. Then, over time, as these properties sell, you will develop a thorough and accurate selection of comparables.

Just as importantly, tracking sales will help you discover what features create the most market appeal, the quickest sales, and the steepest price premiums. With such thorough market knowledge, you will instantly recognize when properties that hit the market are priced below their market value. If you lack ready knowledge, that great bargain-priced property will probably be sold before you're informed enough to act.

You also will be able to use such factual market knowledge to support your offers and purchase (or sales) negotiations (selected and interpreted in your favor, of course). Persuading with facts wins more negotiations than "That's my offer. Take it or leave it."

Let's now go through the comp sale points of comparison in more detail. As you can see, the blanks provided on the appraisal form in Figure 14.1 do not provide much room for explanation or critical differentiation. That's one reason why professional appraisers often err in their judgments. Typically, they paint with a broad brush and in doing so miss details that can make a noteworthy difference.

In addition, you may be surprised to learn that, more often than not, appraisers have never seen the insides of their comp properties. At best, they try to obtain such information second-hand from the sales agents who were involved in the transactions. Alternatively (and I have seen this in too many reports to count), appraisers make stuff up or simply ignore major differences among comp and subject properties because the appraisers lack knowledge that such differences exist.

For these and other reasons, I assure you that neither I nor Donald Trump relies on appraisers or real estate agents to tell us what a property is worth. We listen, we review, we critique, and then we decide for ourselves. You should too.

Address and Proximity to Subject

As a rule, the closer your comp properties are to your subject property, the better. (In fact, ideally, for any given appraisal, you want your comp properties to match your subject property in every way that's possible.) Too often, appraisers pick comps that sit too far from the subject.

What's "too far"? Any distance that places the comp property in a different zone of desirability. It could be on the wrong side of a border street, in a different school district, or farther from the subway or el train. Always drive by the comps that an appraiser selects. Are the locations truly comparable? Are the features of the location similar in every material respect?

Sales Price and Price Per Square Foot

Generally, investors and mortgage lenders like to see the value of a subject property come in at least 10 to 20 percent below the top end of the neighborhood price range. Properties priced at or below the prevailing price range of a neighborhood tend to show better marketability.

In addition, if you can't find comps that perfectly match the subject (which is quite likely), select comps that rank both superior and inferior to the subject. That way you can bracket the value of the subject and give yourself a more definitive estimate. When all comps ran superior (or inferior) to the subject, you will find it more difficult to answer "how much less" or "how much more" the subject property is worth.

For example, say, superior properties have recently sold at around $450,000 to $475,000 and inferior properties have sold for $400,000 to $420,000. By bracketing the subject property, you know that its market value lies between $425,000 and $445,000. You've narrowed your range of value.

As we've noted before, price per square foot provides a useful rule of thumb to estimate market value. To calculate price per square foot (p.s.f.), simply divide sales price (less concessions, if any; see the following equation) of a property by its gross living area. (Do not count garages, basements, attics, storage sheds, and so on.) For example, assume a property sold at a price of $380,000 and includes 1,843 square feet of living space:

$$\text{p.s.f.} = \frac{\$380,000}{1,843}$$

$$\text{p.s.f.} = \$206$$

Price per square foot gives you a ballpark starting figure, but, as you have seen, never give it the final say until you've thoroughly compared and evaluated property features.

Data Sources and Verification

In a minority of appraisals, appraisers will cite personal inspection as a data source for comps. Much more often, appraisers will cite public records, multiple listing service, and real estate agents. Although no appraiser (or inspector) could work without relying on secondhand data, always verify from several sources. Secondhand data multiply the possibilities for error.

Value Adjustments

On the appraisal form in Figure 14.1, you now come to a list of features. Because no subject property could ever match the comp properties with respect to every feature, market value estimates require you to "adjust" the price of the comps according to how their features differ from the subject property.

In other words, the adjustment process answers this question: At what price would the comp property had sold had its features mirrored the subject's features? To figure the answer to this question, you compare the subject property to each comp—feature by feature. If the properties match, no adjustment is necessary.

If the comp is superior, then to make it equivalent to the subject, the estimated value of its feature advantage is *subtracted* from the comp's selling price. Conversely, if the subject stands superior to a comp on a specific feature, the estimated value of that disadvantage is *added* to its sales price. In this way, the adjusted sales price for each comparable fairly indicates the market value of the subject property.

Refer to Table 14.1, and we will illustrate this adjustment process through a simple example.

In the Comp 1 sale, the sellers carried back a 90 percent LTV mortgage (10 percent down) on the property at an interest rate of 6.5 percent. At the time, investor financing usually required a 75 percent LTV (25 percent down) and a 7.5 percent interest rate on this type of property. Without this favorable owner financing, Comp 1 would

Table 14.1 Adjustment Process (Selected Features)

	Comp 1	Comp 2	Comp 3
Sales price	$225,120	$213,440	$211,060
Features			
Sales concessions	Similar	−7,500	Similar
Financing concessions	−11,250	Similar	Similar
Date of sale	Similar	+7,500	Similar
Location	Similar	Similar	−15,000
Floor plan (design)	Similar	+3,750	Similar
Garage	+8,250	Similar	+12,750
Pool, patio, deck	−6,750	−9,750	Similar
Adjusted sales price of comparables	$215,370	$207,440	$208,810

probably have sold for $11,250 less than its actual sales price of $225,120. Because the definition of market value requires financing on terms typically available in the market, the premium created by this OWC (owner will carry) financing had to be subtracted from Comp 1's sales price. Here are the explanations for several other adjustments:

Comp 1 Garage at (+) $8,250: The subject property has an oversized double-car garage, but Comp 1 only has a single-car garage. With a better garage like the subject's, Comp 1 would have brought a $8,250 higher sales price.

Comp 1 Pool, Patio, and Deck at (−) $6,750: Comp 1 is superior to the subject property on this feature because the subject lacks a deck and tile patio. Without this feature, Comp 1 would have sold for $6,750 less.

Comp 2 Date of Sale: Market value presumes current sales comparison data. Because Comp 2 sold six months earlier in a rising market, it would likely sell at a price $7,500 higher today.

Comp 2 Sales Concession at (−) $7,500: The $213,440 sales price in this transaction included the seller's custom-made drapes, a washer and dryer, and a storage shed. Because these items aren't customary in this market, the sales price had to be adjusted downward to equalize this feature with the subject property, the sale of which will not include these items.

Comp 2 Floor Plan (Design) at (+) $3,750: Unlike the subject property, this house lacked convenient access from the garage to the kitchen. The garage was built under the house, and residents had to carry groceries up an outside stairway to enter the kitchen. With more conventional access, the selling price of Comp 2 would probably have increased by $3,750.

Comp 3 Location at (−) $15,000: This house was located on a cul-de-sac and its backyard bordered an environmentally protected wooded area. In contrast, the subject property sits on a typical subdivision street, and its rear yard abuts that of a neighbor. Because of this favored feature, the subject property could be expected to sell for $15,000 less than Comp 3.

After adjusting for inferior and superior features (or concessions), you then total each column of figures. This number tells you the sales price each comp would have commended if it had been a clone of the subject property. You may now wonder, "How can I come up with the specific dollar amounts for each of the adjustments?" To that question, there's no easy answer. It comes from the knowledge you will gain by tracking many sales transactions over a period of months or even years. You also draw on the knowledge of professionally competent real estate agents and appraisers.

Yet, even if you lack experience, critically assess the opinions of the pros against your own judgments. Ask questions. Explore their reasoning. Verify their facts. As you look at properties, educate yourself to identify the features that could make a difference. Remember, you closely inspect and evaluate not merely to estimate market value. You also are imagining ways to add value to the property.

Transfer (Sales) History

During the late 1980s, some property markets crashed. This bust bankrupted many banks and savings and loan associations. A post-mortem of this bust showed that these property markets had been plagued by flipping, fraud, and speculation. Consequently, regulators of financial institutions now require appraisers to investigate the frequency of past sales transactions for both the subject and the comps.

Properties that get flipped frequently at higher and higher prices often signal a property market that may be heading for a downturn. When regulators see such signals, they urge mortgage lenders to tighten their credit standards and appraise properties and LTV ratios with more caution.

Likewise, you should show similar restraint. Or, if you wish to play the flipping game, sharpen your skills of market timing. Such skills become ever more critical to your success and solvency.

(In this sense, I refer primarily to speculative flippers, not investors who buy properties for renovation and resale.)

Indicated Value by Sales Comparison Approach

After you compare concessions, sales dates, features, and transfer history, you are ready to make an *informed judgment* about the market value of the subject property. Although many people claim to know property values, only a thorough methodology with accurate data can give you the confidence to act quickly (when desirable) without commensurate risk.

The Cost Approach

Although many residential market value appraisals do not require the cost (and income) approaches for the reasons cited, as an investor, you should always stay closely informed about a property's cost of reconstruction.

Calculate the Cost to Build New

To see the methodology of the cost approach, refer to the lower half of page 240, Figure 14.1. First, you calculate how much it would cost to build the property using the dollars-per-square-foot construction costs that would apply in your area for the type of property you're valuing.

As you see, replacement cost is figured from the size and quality of the building. Be sure to account for the cost of any upgrades and extras (e.g., crystal chandelier, high-grade wall-to-wall carpeting, Subzero appliances or Kohler plumbing fixtures, sauna, or hot tub) as well as a swimming pool, garage, carport, patios, porches, and so on. Then add these extras to the basic per-square-foot construction costs.

Subtract Depreciation

After you calculate the cost to reconstruct a property at today's building costs, you take note of three types of depreciation: (1) physical,

(2) functional, and (3) economic (external). An older building is generally worth less than a similarly-built new building because of *physical* depreciation (wear and tear). Properties deteriorate from age, weather, use, and abuse. Frayed carpets, faded paint, cracked plaster, rusty plumbing, and leaky roofs bring down a property's value. How much? That's a judgment call. To fill in a specific number, estimate a percentage for wear and tear relative to new. Usually, "well maintained" might warrant a 10 to 20 percent figure. For really "run down," depreciation could total 50 to 70 percent of new building costs. Instead of applying a percentage depreciation figure, you could also itemize the costs of the repairs and renovations that would put the property in top condition.

After physical depreciation, next estimate the amount of *functional* depreciation. Unlike wear and tear that naturally occurs through use and abuse, functional depreciation refers to a loss of value because of problems such as out-of-favor dark-wood paneling, ill-designed floor plan, low-amperage electrical system, or unpopular color schemes or architectural design. A property may show little wear and tear (physical depreciation) yet still suffer large functional depreciation because the features of the property no longer appeal to a majority of potential buyers or renters.

The Bonwit Teller building—a faux Art Deco box— had outlasted its usefulness. It was functionally obsolete. The site was ready for a higher and more profitable use.

External (locational) depreciation occurs when a property no longer reflects the highest and best use for a site. Say you find a well-kept house located in an area that's now predominantly commercial. Zoning of the site has changed. More than likely, the house would add little or nothing to the site's value. When someone buys the "house," they will tear it down to make way for a new retail store or office building. This same principle applies when neighborhoods move upscale and well-kept, three-bedroom, two-bath houses of

2,000 square feet are torn down and replaced with 6,000-square-foot $2,000,000 (or higher) houses.

Economically obsolete properties are called "teardowns." Keep in mind, though, that the term "teardown" can apply to buildings that display excellent repair as well as to junkers. If you buy a teardown, pay only for lot value less the cost of demolition and removal.

Site Value

To estimate lot value, find similar (vacant) lots that have recently sold or lots that have sold with teardowns on them. To value similar sites, compare features such as size, frontage, views, topography, government regulations, subdivision rules, and other characteristics that buyers look for.

Estimate Market Value (Cost Approach)

As you can see on the appraisal form in Figure 14.1, after these three steps—(1) calculate a property's replacement construction cost as if newly built, (2) subtract depreciation, and (3) add in site value—you have estimated market value. Because it's difficult to precisely measure construction costs, accrued depreciation, and site value, the cost approach never gives a definitive answer. But in addition to helping you forecast price trends, it provides a figure to check against the comparable sales approach and the income approach.

The Income Approach (GRM)

Just below the section "Cost Approach to Value" on the appraisal form in Figure 14.1, notice an entry labeled "Income Approach to Value." That type of income approach refers to an appraisal technique called the *gross rent multiplier* (GRM).

To calculate market value using the GRM, you need to discover the monthly rents and sales prices of similar houses or apartment buildings. Say that you learn of the following sales of rental houses: (1) 214 Jackson was rented at $1,250 a month and sold for $220,000, (2) 312 Lincoln was rented at $1,350 a month and sold for $247,000, and (3) 107 Adams was rented at $1,175 a month and sold for $210,000. With this information, you can calculate a range of GRMs for this neighborhood:

$$GRM = \frac{\text{Sales price}}{\text{Monthly rent}}$$

Property	Sales Price	Monthly Rent	GRM
214 Jackson	$220,000	÷ $ 1,250	= 176
312 Lincoln	247,000	÷ 1,350	= 183
107 Adams	210,000	÷ 1,175	= 179

If the house you are valuing could rent for $1,225 a month, figure the appropriate GRM from your comps as follows:

Subject House (Estimated Value Range)

GRM	Monthly Rent	Value
176	× $1,225	= $215,600
183	× 1,225	= 224,175
179	× 1,225	= 219,275

The value would range from $215,600 to $224,175.

Because the GRM method does not directly adjust for sales or financing concessions, features, location, condition, or operating expenses, this technique "roughly" estimates market value. Nevertheless, many investors use it as a first-pass indicator. Similar to the price-per-square-foot comp sales approach, the GRM works best when you find quite similar rental properties in the same neighborhood.

The GRMs shown in these examples *do not necessarily* correspond to the GRMs that would apply in your city. *Even within the same city,* different neighborhoods will show wide differences in their typical GRMs. In the San Diego area, GRMs for single-family homes in La Jolla could range upward of 400; in nearby Clairemont, you may find GRMs in the 250 to 300 range; and in National City, GRMs may drop below 200. Even within the same neighborhood, GRMs for single-family houses often run higher than those of condominiums. As with all appraisal methods, use the relevant *local* data before you apply GRMs.

You can get killed paying top dollar for a superb location. Or by buying a poor location, even at a low price. You've got to know the value of the deal. Never pay more than the deal is worth.

Reconciliation of Value Estimates

Once you've completed all three approaches to value, you next weigh your results according to the relevance and applicability to the problem under study. As noted, for single-family homes, the comp sales approach provides the best guide to market value. However, for investment properties—although the basic appraisal principles remain the same—the specific comp sale and income techniques differ somewhat from those approaches we just reviewed.

Valuing Income Properties

To briefly illustrate how to value an income property, we will look at the 20-year-old Royal Terrace apartment complex. Royal Terrace consists of 38 efficiency apartments that each measures 550 square feet in size. This property is located in Middleton, Iowa, a low-cost midwestern city that offers economic stability but little or no job, income, or population growth.

After closely examining the physical features, location, and services of Royal Terrace, you were quite fortunate to find in the same neighborhood two similar properties that had sold within the past six months. Data on these comparables are as follows.

2735 Maple (Comparable No. 1)

This building is 25 years old and contains 33 efficiency apartments. It shows more wear and tear than the subject, but otherwise it's comparable in construction and condition. One major disadvantageous feature, though: it's located directly across from a new high school. Its units are presently rented at $285 per month, and each unit contains 525 square feet. Information obtained from the property manager shows that vacancy in the building has been stable at about 4 percent and that operating expenses are at 52 percent of gross potential income. Public records and talks with real estate agents revealed that this property sold with a 20 percent down payment and a 25-year fixed-rate mortgage at 7.0 percent interest. The price was $506,700.

1460 Elm (Comparable No. 2)

This building is 16 years old and contains 40 efficiency apartments. It's a little better constructed than the subject, and it's only two blocks away from a neighborhood park with tennis courts, pool, and a nine-hole golf course. The units are presently rented at $315 per month, and like the subject, each contains 550 square feet. Vacancies are averaging 4 percent, and as a proportion of gross potential income, operating expenses total 49 percent. Public records show that the property was financed with an 80 percent LTV ratio mortgage for 30 years at 6.75 percent interest. The selling price was $772,400.

In addition to the comp sale data, you consulted several recent construction contracts and referred to the *Marshall and Swift Valuation Service*. From this research, you estimated that inclusive construction costs for a building like the subject would today run about $72 per square foot.

From the Royal Terrace owner's bookkeeper, you obtained the following income and expense data for the calendar year ended this past December 31.

GRM

The GRM technique is used for income properties in much the same way as it is for rental houses and condominium units. From market comparables, you calculate a gross income multiplier. Then you multiply that figure by the subject property's gross potential income. However, for rental houses and condominiums, it's customary to calculate the multiplier on the basis of gross monthly rentals. For apartment buildings, the GRM is calculated on an annual basis. Consider that the GRMs for our two comparables are 4.49 (506,700/112,860) and 5.10 (772.400/151,200). If, say, you decide on a 4.75 multiplier for Royal Terrace, its indicated market value using the GRM technique would equal $638,970:

$$4.75 \times \$134,520 = \$638,970$$

The GRM is used extensively in some areas and for certain types of apartment buildings. But in general, buyers do not assign it as much importance as direct income capitalization. Unless the selected comparables are very much alike, the GRM provides too crude a measure. In addition, buyers seldom use the GRM to value office buildings, shopping centers, and other types of income properties. Because of wide differences in lease provisions as well as property features, the GRM would omit too many important details. Nevertheless, the GRM is another tool that you can work with when it reflects typical investor sentiment.

Income Capitalization

Another income valuation approach that you should apply to multiple-unit income properties (but may also be used to value smaller properties) is called direct income capitalization. Recall that to calculate market value with the direct capitalization method, you use the following formula:

$$V = \frac{NOI}{R}$$

Here, V represents the value to be estimated, NOI represents the net operating income of the property, and R represents the overall rate of return on capital (i.e., the capitalization, or, for short, the cap rate) that buyers of similar income properties typically require.

Thus, if Royal Terrace is expected to earn an NOI of $63,174 per year and the applicable cap rate is 0.096, you calculate this property's value as follows:

$$V = \frac{63,174}{0.096}$$

$$V = \$658,062$$

Of course, this simple calculation leaves unanswered the questions of how to compute NOI and R. We now turn to these issues.

NOI

Investors define NOI as annual gross potential rental income from a property less vacancy and collection losses, operating expenses, replacement reserves, property taxes, and property and liability insurance.

However, as is the case for the owner of Royal Terrace, many nonprofessional investors (as well as bookkeepers or accountants) do not know how to construct an NOI statement for purposes of income capitalization.

In addition, many knowledgeable owners of income properties purposely overstate their rental income collections and understate their vacancies and operating expenses. By distorting income and expenses in this way, these owners try to persuade you that their properties earn more and thus are worth more than is really justified by the *facts*.

Therefore, whether you're buying from amateurs or pros, caveat emptor. Never casually accept the numbers they give you. Instead, reconstruct the NOI figures from your own research and market knowledge.

Now, let's turn to the owners' and the reconstructed income statements for Royal Terrace (Tables 14.2 and 14.3). You know that an appraiser must reconstruct the owner's income statement to reflect the principles discussed here. This reconstruction more accurately reflects the NOI the property can be expected to earn under competent management during the coming year.

Reconstruct Income: First notice that to reconstruct effective gross income, we used market rental and vacancy rates—not those actually experienced by the subject property. To find out what rent and vacancy levels were reasonable, consider the rent levels of the selected comparable properties as well as the rents achieved by other neighborhood apartment buildings. You must rely on a current market analysis. With income recalculated, we next reconstruct a variety of expense items.

Management and Promotion: In the owner's statement, no allowance was made for either management or promotion. The owner had self-managed the building, and because of the relatively low rental rates, he always enjoyed a waiting list just through word of mouth. A new owner, though, would expect to incur both management and promotional expenses.

Insurance and Property Taxes: The insurance amount in the owner's statement errs because it wasn't prorated over the full three years of coverage. The actual amount should have been one-third of $19,200, or $6,400. We also must adjust the expense amounts reported by the owner's accountant for property taxes. Partially, the increase in property taxes was figured to reflect

Table 14.2 Royal Terrace Owner-Prepared Income Statement

Actual rents collected[1]		$123,120
Expenses		
Property insurance (three-year policy)	$19,200	
Property taxes (pd. 2/8/86 for year 1985)	3,682	
Caretaker salary	12,000	
Gas and electric	16,590	
Water and sewage	3,200	
Trash collection	1,847	
Repairs and maintenance	4,383	
Mortgage interest	18,390	
Depreciation	15,444	94,736
Net income		$28,384

[1]At nearly 100% occupancy.

Table 14.3 Your Reconstructed Royal Terrace Income Statement

Gross potential income (38 × 12 × $295)	$134,520
Vacancy and collection @ 4%	5,381
Effective gross income (123,120)	$129,139
Expenses[1]	
Property management (0)	5,165
Promotion and advertising (0)	600
Property insurance (19,200)	6,400
Property taxes (3,682)	6,500
Caretaker salary (12,000)	9,000
Gas and electric (16,590)	18,900
Water and sewage (3,200)	3,800
Trash collection (1,847)	2,100
Repairs, maintenance, and reserves (4,383)	11,500
Miscellaneous	2,000
Total expenses	$65,965
Net operating income	$63,174

[1] Owner's reported income and expense amounts are shown in parenthesis. For purposes of market value appraisals, depreciation and mortgage interest are not included in calculating NOI.

the new assessed value that will attach to the property after sale. In this city, the assessor's office gets behind in its appraisal of properties. But when a sale comes through the county records, the assessor picks it up and changes the property's assessed value accordingly. In addition, tax rates have been increased significantly by the county council, so next year's taxes will go up even without a updated tax appraisal of the property.

Utilities, Caretakers, and So On: With respect to utilities and trash collection charges, you should check with the companies that provide these services to the subject property for its usage rates. On the basis of these reported rates, we can compute each of the expense items using the costs effective the coming year. The caretaker's salary expense item was reduced in the reconstructed statement because some of these duties will be performed by the new property management firm.

Upon investigation, you found that the owner routinely performed some repair and maintenance chores around the property. Because a new buyer would purchase Royal Terrace as an investment—and not as a source of self-employment—you should increase this expense amount accordingly.

Repairs, Maintenance, and Reserves for Replacement: Property sellers routinely understate the costs necessary to maintain their properties and replace components (carpets, roof, appliances, and so on) as they wear out. So, we've increased that amount to a level that's more representative of local experience with similar properties.

Miscellaneous Items: As a final item, notice that we added in $2,000 for miscellaneous expenses. These items include costs such as legal and accounting fees, cleaning supplies, and redecorating materials (paint, wallpaper), but we omit the mortgage interest and depreciation expenses that are reported on the owner's income statement. Although interest and depreciation are certainly bona fide ownership expenses, convention dictates that they are not counted as operating expenses for purposes of calculating NOI.

NOI: After all income and expense items are reconstructed, you can see that the NOI for Royal Terrace is estimated for the coming year to equal $63,174.

Deriving Capitalization Rates

In practice, appraisers and investors rely on market-derived capitalization rates. For example, to derive the capitalization rate for Royal Terrace, let's compute rates applied by the buyers of 2735 Maple and 1460 Elm (Table 14.4). For 2735 Maple, a property somewhat inferior to the subject (it's five years older, shows a little more wear, and is located across from Hot Rod High), the buyer applied a capitalization rate of 9.80 percent. For the superior 1460 Elm (it's better located, four years younger, and was financed at 6.75 percent) its buyer applied a capitalization rate of 9.20 percent. Considering these facts, what can we infer with respect to the subject property's capitalization rate?

First, we can see that the subject property's rate most likely will lie between 0.092 and 0.098. The reason is that—all other things being equal—investors typically prefer newer properties to older properties. Often they believe that newer properties that are well-located and in good condition are less risky than older properties. Investors also believe that the income streams of such properties will last longer and are more likely to increase. Because on these criteria the Royal Terrace fits between the two comparables, so will its capitalization rate.

Yet, we need to carry our analysis further and ask whether the subject property lies closest in character to 2735 Maple or 1460

Table 14.4 Deriving a Market-Based Cap Rate

Comparables	NOI	Sales Price	Rate
2735 Maple	$49,658	$506,700	$0.098
1460 Elm	71,064	772,400	0.092
Subject	63,174	?	?

Elm. After we weigh and consider all similarities and differences, we ask, what is the most likely capitalization rate an investor will apply to the Royal Terrace income stream? We need a number.

How about 0.096? Like other decisions in appraisal, selecting a cap rate requires not only facts, but judgment. Remember, no two properties are identical; no two buyers are exactly alike; and no one ever has full market or property information. Here we reasoned that buyers would view Royal Terrace most similar to 2735 Maple. Plus, the subject apartments probably would be financed at 7.0 percent, rather than at the 6.75 percent rate that applied to 1460 Elm. In this instance, and with much deliberation, we choose a market-derived capitalization rate of 0.096.

Direct Capitalization Approach

The final step in the direct capitalization approach to market value requires investors to convert a property's NOI stream into a capital sum. For our example, we perform this step by dividing $63,174 by 0.096. Thus, the indicated market value of the subject property via direct capitalization equals $658,062:

$$V = \frac{63,174}{0.096}$$

$$V = \$658,062$$

Comparable Sales Approach

When they buy apartments, office buildings, and shopping centers, most investors lean heavily on the capitalized income method. However, they will also use some ballpark comp sale figures to verify the reasonableness of their income valuation. For example, they might set up some type of price-per-unit and price-per-square-foot figures as shown in Table 14.5.

Table 14.5 Per-Unit Comparisons

Features	2735 Maple	1460 Elm	Royal Terrace
Physical conditions	Slightly inferior	Somewhat better	Average
Age	25 years	16 years	20 years
Location	More traffic noise	Park nearby	Average
	Inferior	Superior	
Financing	80% LTV	80% LTV	
	7.0% 25 years	6.75% 30 years	
Sales price	$506,700	$772,400	?
No. of suites	33 efficiencies	40 efficiencies	38 efficiencies
No. of rooms	33	40	38
No. of sq.ft.	17,325 sq.ft.	22,000 sq.ft.	20,900 sq.ft.
Price per unit	$15,354	$19,310	$16,800[1]
Price per sq.ft.	$29.25	$35.10	$31.50[1]

[1] We estimated these per-unit amounts after comparing the subject property comparables.

From the data in Table 14.5, we can estimate the market value of Royal Terrace via market comp sales figures as follows:

38 units	×	$16,800 p.p.u.	=	$638,400
20,900 sq. ft.	×	$31.50 p.p.s.f.	=	$658,350

As you can see, these comp sale value estimates tend to support the cap rate approach. Of course, as with all appraisals, you never obtain a precisely correct answer. Facts, interpretations, judgments, and reasoning will differ among investors. You can, though, craft your analyses to raise your probability of making a great decision.

The Cost Approach

As you can see from Table 14.6, the cost approach shows that the property's value equals $922,525.

Table 14.6 The Cost Approach: Royal Terrace

Estimated reproduction costs (20,900 sq. ft. × $72)	$1,504,800
Depreciation	
Physical	$510,275
Functional	$72,000
Locational	$0
Depreciated value of improvements	$822,525
Land value	$100,000
Indicated market value	$922,525

The cost approach shows a value far in excess of the market and income approaches. Why? Because Middleton lacks a dynamic local economy. Building construction costs (which are determined by the national and international prices of materials) have increased faster than properties in Middleton have appreciated.

As a result, the investor who buys Royal Terrace will not likely face much competition from newly constructed apartments or houses. These newer properties must charge much higher rents (or sales prices).

As a result, this investor faces less market risk. In addition, he might also enjoy good opportunities to upgrade and create value for the property. Since investors do not expect properties in Middleton to appreciate much, they can buy at higher cap rates and thus experience larger cash flows per dollar of investment.

All in all, at a price of $650,000 or less, Royal Terrace might prove to be a great investment. But before deciding whether to place an offer, most investors would run the numbers to calculate cash on cash return on investment (ROI) and total return over time—which will include equity buildup through amortization (paying off the mortgage financing) and potential appreciation.

Cash on Cash Return on Investment

For purposes of illustration, let's say you buy Royal Terrace at a price of $650,000. To complete your purchase, you invest $130,000 cash out of pocket (20 percent down payment) and you borrow $520,000 (80 percent LTV) at 7 percent for 30 years. Accordingly, to calculate your first year, before tax cash flow (BTCF) subtract your annual mortgage payments from your first year expected NOI.

NOI	$63,174
Annual Mortgage Payment	$41,905
($520,000 @ 7%, 30 years)	

$$\text{BTCF} = \$21,269$$

Next, to calculate your first year cash on cash ROI, you divide your out-of-pocket cash investment (down payment) of $130,000 into your BTCF.

$$\text{ROI} = \frac{\text{BTCF}}{\text{cash investment}}$$

$$\text{ROI} = \frac{\$21,269}{\$130,000}$$

$$\text{ROI} = 16.3\%$$

Therefore, based on these figures (and providing your market and property analysis support such numbers), your cash on cash ROI looks pretty good. Through leverage, you have increased the property's return from 9.6 percent (the cap rate equals the pretax, prefinancing ROI) to 16.3 percent. In today's marketplace, most investors would find a 16.3 percent cash on cash ROI quite attractive.

Total Return on Investment

The above cash on cash return, though, does not include the additional benefits that you would achieve from amortization and property appreciation. To calculate your total return on investment (TROI), you need to project your annual BTCF over your expected period of ownership (say five years) and the cash proceeds that you will gain from a sale of the property.

To illustrate, assume that because Middleton lacks dynamic economic growth, Royal Terrace BTCFs increase just 2 percent per year, and similarly, the property appreciates just 2 percent a year. After five years, your mortgage balance will have fallen from $530,000 to $488,343.

Now, refer to Tables 14.7 and 14.8. First, you can see that a 2 percent rate of appreciation gives you a net proceeds of sale (after deducting 5 percent of the selling price to cover the sales expense) of $193,427. Table 14.7 also shows the net sale of proceeds that would result if the property incurred no appreciation (pessimistic view) or 5 percent appreciation (optimistic view).

Using an Excel spreadsheet (or similar software), you can next generate your total return on investment figures, such as those shown in Table 14.8.

Under the varying rates of appreciation, the expected TROI for Royal Terrace ranges from a low of 17.78 percent to a high of 31.67 percent.

The figures in Table 14.8, of course, represent just a few of the results that spreadsheet software permits you to easily calculate. You could also vary rates of growth for rents and operating expenses, changes in mortgage interest rates, mortgage term, amount of down

Table 14.7 Net Proceeds of Sale of Property at Different Appreciation Rates

Property appreciation	0%	2%	5%
Sales price	$650,000	$717,653	$829,583
Less 5% sales expense	$32,500	$35,883	$41,479
Less mtg. balance	$488,343	$488,343	$488,343
Net proceeds of sale (pretax)	$129,157	$193,427	$299,761

Table 14.8 TROI Calculation Using BTCF Increases of 2 Percent per Year with Different Rates of Property Appreciation

	Year 0	Year 1	Year 2	Year 3	Year 4	Year 5	TROI
Before tax cash flow (BTCF)		$21,269	$22,425	$23,600	$24,793	$26,006	
No appreciation	($130,000)	$21,269	$22,425	$23,600	$24,793	$129,157	
						$155,163	17.78%
Before tax cash flow (BTCF)		$21,269	$22,425	$23,600	$24,793	$26,006	
2% appreciation	($130,000)	$21,269	$22,425	$23,600	$24,793	$193,427	
						$219,433	23.86%
Before tax cash flow (BTCF)		$21,269	$22,425	$23,600	$24,793	$26,006	
5% appreciation	($130,000)	$21,269	$22,425	$23,600	$24,793	$299,761	
						$325,767	31.67%

payment, and any other variables you wish to examine. Naturally, too, you can use spreadsheets to value the returns that your entrepreneurial improvements can generate.

By running many scenario analyses, you can construct a series of potential outcomes that range from worst case to best case. Because no one can precisely forecast the future, understanding a full range of possibilities will not only help you make better decisions, it will help you anticipate and manage those periods when fate turns against you.

CONCLUSION

Congratulations. You now possess more knowledge about real estate investing than the great majority of investors who have owned properties for years. Even better, you are learning to think like an entrepreneur. You know that real estate always offers grand opportunities for those individuals who train themselves to read, listen, and seek out new places and new ideas.

Donald Trump has remarked, "Sometimes I'm hard on people because I know they can do more, and I know they haven't lived up to their potential. I want to become the spark that fires them up to reach and achieve in ways that I know they can. History shows that those who persist succeed. Respect yourself enough to take advantage of the possibilities and promises that await you. I expect you to succeed, and will accept no excuses."

You have gained the knowledge. You have gained the entrepreneurial mindset. Now it's up to you to act. Think 5, 10, 20 years into the future. Where do you want to be? You can make it happen.

Mr. Trump and I want you to prosper for yourself, for your family, and for those you serve. We wish you good fortune. Please let us know how you're doing. You can contact me directly at geldred@trumpuniversity.com.

INDEX